Mick and The Cleaner

National Library of Australia
Cataloguing-in-Publication entry

Creator: Staples, Peter J., author.
Title: Mick and The Cleaner/Peter Staples; Geoff Slattery, editor.
ISBN: 9780987342881 (paperback)
Subjects: Burles, Mick.
The Cleaner (Race horse)
Horse trainers--Australia--Biography.
Horses--Training--Australia.
Race horses--Australia--Biography.
Horse racing--Australia.
Other Creators/Contributors: Slattery, Geoff, editor.
Dewey Number: 798.2092

Group Publisher: Geoff Slattery
Project Manager: Marlo Mercuri
Editor: Geoff Slattery
Designer: Chris Downey
Cover Design: Chris Downey

Printed and bound in Australia by McPherson's Printing Group

The Slattery Media Group Pty Ltd
1 Albert Street, Richmond, Victoria, Australia 3121
www.slatterymedia.com

Mick and The Cleaner

PETER STAPLES

FOREWORD BY

Lee Freedman

About the Author

PETER Staples was born in Melbourne where he spent his teenage years as a budding musician before eventually making his way to Tasmania in 1982, where he has carved out a stellar career as a sports journalist.

He quickly found a niche, writing about racing a niche that took him to the role of chief racing writer with Hobart's daily metropolitan newspaper, *The Mercury*.

His first venture as an author came in the late 1990s when he wrote Australian Test captain Ricky Ponting's first book, *Punter—First Test of a Champion* (Pan MacMillan, 1998).

Since 2004 he has been a member of the selection panel of the Australian Thoroughbred Racing Hall of Fame and he is the face of Tasmanian racing via his role as a presenter with Sky Channel.

He has been the company journalist with the Tasmanian Racing Industry's governing body since 2002 and more recently he returned to *The Mercury* as a daily contributor on all things racing.

I dedicate this to my late mother Gladys Staples-Kelly who encouraged me to pursue my dream—we got there, Mum.

Thanks

Thanks to Mick Burles for allowing me into his private life and for delivering the warts and all truth of his remarkable journey.

A special thanks to Carissa Burles and Kim Burles for being so brutally honest.

And a big thank you to my wife Linda for being so patient, helpful and understanding throughout the project that we titled TBB (The Bloody Book).

Contents

Foreword

By Australian Racing Hall of Fame Trainer Lee Freedman

I was sitting in a pub one Sunday afternoon having a meal with some friends and I was watching a race in Tassie and saw this horse they called The Cleaner win a race by an incredible margin and he did it leading throughout.

I was so impressed by the horse's win I followed it up and found out that Mick Burles was the trainer so when he eventually came across to Melbourne I made a point of introducing myself and we just struck a chord.

I was interested in what he had to say and he was only too pleased to pick my brain about a few things and the relationship grew from there.

Mick is a salt-of-the-earth type of bloke who calls a spade a spade but he's obviously a very talented horseman. To be able to train a horse on a tiny country track in Tasmania and get him into two Cox Plates is enough proof that he can train; but what he does have is that special something only the top trainers possess.

For blokes like Mick these outstanding horses don't come along every day but a trainer has to be good enough to identify the talent and then get the best results from their charge, which is why what he has achieved with The Cleaner must be applauded.

He's been able to play with the big boys and more than hold his own with a horse that obviously had an ability that, in those early times, only Mick could see.

I thought it was very sad when I heard that the owners of The Cleaner had decided to send the horse to another trainer but when you play in this game you have to be prepared for setbacks. It's just part and parcel of the industry in which we live and work.

Mick calls it as he sees it and no doubt he was upset when the horse left his yard but he's a tough old bugger and he'll get on with life and that's another thing I admire about the man.

In this industry you meet all sorts of characters and Mick Burles is one of the more colourful. As a horseman his track record speaks for itself but more importantly he is a terrific bloke who possesses a great sense of humour. God knows that's something we all need in this game.

Lee Freedman
August 2016

Prologue

Racing stardom, at least in Australia, is not only the domain of the rich and famous. Through generations a battling trainer, or owner, often with an unlikely galloper has made it to the top of the tree. Through the 2000s it was Takeover Target and his former taxi driver-cum-trainer Joe Janiak. Then came Mick Burles and The Cleaner, whose successive wins in the Group 3 Dato Tan Chin Nam Stakes at Moonee Valley gave the duo a well-earned place in two W. S. Cox Plates (2014-15).

More than that, The Cleaner was the first Tasmanian-trained horse to grace Australasia's most prestigious Group 1 middle distance weight-for-age event. For Mick Burles, The Cleaner's knockabout trainer, it was a dream come true.

For more than two years, Mick and his gallant galloper captured the imagination of punters around Australia. The Cleaner's rise through the ranks was amazing given his start to racing in Tasmania had promised little more than the possibility of winning a few races in restricted classes.

The Cleaner, a $10,000 purchase, became a crowd favourite through his courageous front-running catch-me-if-you-can style of racing. Once unleashed on Melbourne metropolitan tracks, he delivered knockout blows to some of the turf's most expensive and high-profiled gallopers.

Racing has a knack of finding unlikely heroes and The Cleaner and his trainer/mate were the perfect fits for such roles.

Phar Lap gave an entire nation something to cheer about during the Great Depression (1929-1932) and there have since been numerous racing superstars who have won the hearts of millions including Rising Fast, Tulloch, Vain, Kingston Town, Makybe Diva and Black Caviar. The Cleaner did not have their talent, but he had mass appeal, and he had a trainer whose path to the top was littered with stops and starts and unlikely dreams.

Until The Cleaner came along, Mick was just an ordinary bloke who'd been through life's mill, most recently busting his balls trying to get his moderate team to win maidens and class ones in a state where the racing industry verged on being reduced to little more than a cottage industry.

Mick is a survivor in a rough 'n' tumble game that can turn paupers into millionaires and drag the rich and famous to their knees. He has tasted life as a cellar dweller, has endured a debilitating illness, but, for a fleeting moment, during The Cleaner's heyday, experienced life as one of the elite—until his one good horse was snatched from his grasp.

But the thread that holds him together is the hope that one day he might find another to match the deeds of his best mate—'Bill', aka The Cleaner.

WHETHER that new dream will come true is in the hands of the gods, but whatever fortune—good or bad—comes across his path, Mick can look back on a life well lived.

Mick was in his early teens when one of his school teachers told him his life wouldn't amount to much. He predicted that unless his attitude changed, Mick would have little to offer in the big world and that he should expect no more than to spend his working life as a labourer—at best.

That harsh criticism didn't bother the brash teenager who had a grand plan already mapped out for life beyond his schooldays. Mick was your typical country lad who lived for his sport and any other of the many leisure activities that go hand in hand with living on a farm in a rural community. Mick's grand plan was to be good enough to one day to play football for his beloved Hawthorn and then play and coach in Tasmania when his League career was over.

Mick's elite footy dream never eventuated but his love of Aussie Rules never waned and he did manage to make his mark in the game at a much lower level. He played and coached a total of 494 games with various Tasmanian clubs, spanning from the Tasman Peninsula in the south to Penguin on the north-west Coast. But it was to be his foray into horse racing that eventually found him fame, without the fortune, courtesy of his star racehorse The Cleaner.

Mick endured a rollercoaster ride that would take him on a journey usually reserved for the industry's elite but like all trainers Mick knew his time in the racing spotlight would be limited. During countless interviews, several attempts were made to delve into Mick's identity but he had the knack of fending off personal questions while redirecting the discussion towards the horse. Despite his larger than life character, Mick is a private person, although he is only too happy to spin a bawdy yarn or two at a racing function. Until now he has been reluctant to allow anyone into his private life.

Mick has encountered many setbacks but each time he has managed to regroup and soldier on, just like he was taught to do when he was growing up.

"Life's like a game of cards," he says, "you just have to be happy with the hand you're dealt. We all get curve balls thrown at us, some more than others, but in the end you just have to keep moving forward. I've lived by that philosophy all my life. Some things are harder than others to accept but we can either roll over and take it up the arse or take it on the chin like a man and move on."

Peter Staples
August 2016

1

The Beginning

MICK Burles spent his formative years raising hell wherever and whenever he could in the tiny hamlet of Stormlea, about 100 kilometres south-west of Hobart on Tasmania's picturesque Tasman Peninsula. He was delivered naturally on April 21,1949 at the Koonya District Hospital that accommodated fewer than a dozen beds with usually no more staff than a day surgeon, nurse and an admissions clerk who would double as a general dogsbody.

Mick was the youngest son of four children born to Horace and Valerie Grace Burles and they first lived in a home perched at the top of a hill that overlooks the penal settlement at Port Arthur. Mick hadn't reached his fourth birthday when the family made their way to a small 40-hectare farm at Stormlea.

Stormlea is situated about 20 kilometres south-east of Port Arthur and close to Cape Raoul on the southernmost point of the Tasman Peninsula that marks the entrance to Storm Bay, the gateway to the final run home for competitors in the annual Sydney to Hobart yacht race.

This farm at Stormlea was hardly commercial, but two dairy cows and a multitude of vegetable patches that required daily care and management, allowed for self-sufficiency—at worst.

The property was owned by Mick's maternal grandmother Sissy Nichols (nee Spaulding), a relation of Truganini, presumed to be the last known full-blood Aborigine to die on the island (in May, 1876). Sissy Nichols is listed as a descendant of a sibling of Truganini.

The Nichols-Burles household possessed one of more than 300 dairy licences issued in the state at the time with most farms in the region capable of producing between one and 10 40-litre cans of milk or cream a day with the Burles family lot capable of delivering two cans of full cream on a regular basis. Stormlea was a quiet village and considered a remote location but the soil was fertile and the region produced some of the best dairy and beef cattle on the island.

Mick's future was cast in stone long before he knew he would wander into the world of horse racing. It was his love and admiration of horses from an early age that would eventually take him on the ride of his life.

"Horses have always been a part of my existence," Mick said.

"When I was a kid I had a draft horse named Tom and he was pretty much my horse from the day I first jumped on. I got on really well with Tom but I loved all horses and they got on well with me. I could never resist the temptation to go and pat a horse that was standing near a paddock fence on my way to school; but all the kids who I grew up with were the same. It was just our way of life."

Mick's recollections of his early childhood are mostly memories of what most country boys did to fill in their days in the 1950s. Home duties were paramount and that involved milking the cows morning and night as well as tending to the veggie patches on a rotation basis with his older sister Rhonda.

"I was raised to appreciate the land and all things on it and in it. I'm sure I was no different from any other boy my age in the district but I probably got up to a bit more mischief than most. I guess to some I was a prick of a kid. I loved practical jokes and my favourite pastime was tormenting my sister."

His fondest memories of his childhood centred around his grandmother Sissy Nichols or "Nan" as he always called her. Mick has always been aware of his Aboriginal background however, as his late teens loomed he started to realise that it was more prudent to hide the fact. In the early 1900s in Tasmania those who had Aboriginal blood could either boast it and suffer the consequences or keep their mouths shut. Even up to the time Mick was born and through to the early 1960s any claim of Aboriginality led to contempt and discrimination and Mick was advised by his mum and his grandmother, more than once, to keep his secret close to his chest.

"Although I was taught to be proud I had Aboriginal heritage it wasn't always advisable to tell people I was part blackfella. Mum and Nan talked a lot about us being part Aboriginal and we were taught to be proud of our heritage. Nan used to tell us stories of what life was like when she was a kid growing up. I don't know how many brothers and sisters she had but I know she had 14 children and you could easily see they were Aboriginal.

"Nan's sons, uncle Art and uncle Trevor were both regular visitors to our place at Stormlea and they were as black as the ace of spades. Although I can't remember anything specific that she told me, she made me feel that I was a part of something special even though I didn't know exactly what it was.

"I just wish I'd taken more notice of the things she used to tell us kids because I'm damned sure they'd make good stories today. Nan was fantastic to us kids. Whenever I think of my early childhood and all the good times it usually involved her."

Mick was a natural bushman and he is sure his affinity with nature stems from his heritage and his upbringing.

"I learned a lot about the bush from Nan. She was raised on the land and we'd spend a bit of time wandering the area setting snares for rabbits and she'd tell me stuff that I couldn't learn at school, or anywhere else for that matter. She was bush smart and what she didn't know about the land wasn't worth knowing. When I used to go bush for a few days

I instinctively knew my way back home and I didn't have to be taught to navigate my way around the bush—I just knew."

By the time Mick was old enough to go to school he was well versed in the art of living off the land.

"My life might have been basic by some standards but what we had as kids growing up was far more beneficial than what the city kids had. We were taught that we could live off the land and that whatever we needed to survive was right there in front of us. Nan was always telling us that we should be thankful for what we had."

"We didn't have a television at home until I was about 14, so us kids had to make our own fun and that was the beauty of growing up where I did. I reckon if the kids of today didn't have computers and these bloody fancy iPhones and the like, they'd be a hell of a lot better off—I'm bloody sure of it.

"I had a great life when I was growing up on the farm and while I probably never fully appreciated it back then, I know that if I had the chance to do it all over again I'd want exactly what I had as a kid." He paused and added, "With maybe a couple of things changed slightly."

Mick hadn't reached his first birthday when his father up and left, leaving his mother and Sissy to raise the children.

"I never knew my father although I found out a long time ago that he was living in Hobart and that my eldest brother Robert had gone to live with him. I met up with Robert once when I was about 16 when he wandered into the Port Arthur pub where I was working as an apprentice chef but I never saw him again and I had no interest in meeting my natural father."

Mick's mother had a hard life having been married at a young age. Mick never knew what made his mother appear depressed a lot of the time during his formative years but he was not interested in getting to the core of the problem once the age of innocence was behind him.

"I have fond memories of my mother but when she remarried, nearly all of her attention was focused on my stepdad Tony Arnold. I was about five when Tony came into our lives. One day he just turned up with Mum and she said he was our new father and that was that."

With their mother obviously focused on building her relationship with the new man in her life Mick and Rhonda were pretty much tended to by their grandmother. "It didn't bother me or Rhonda because we had Nan, who pretty much raised us."

Mick's family was disjointed—to say the least. Third-born son Denis was adopted out not long after Mick was born.

"My brother Denis was adopted by the local school bus driver Robert Woolley who lived at Port Arthur. Denis and I went to the same school but we weren't in the same class because he was older. We used to get along well and played football together at school but he wasn't allowed to socialise with me or the rest of the family. I asked Denis a few times to come to my house but he said he wasn't allowed and I never found out why."

Mick refused to ask his mother or grandmother why Denis was adopted out.

"I didn't ask why Denis wasn't living with us because I didn't think it was the right thing to do. I thought Mum and Nan were both protective about it so I just let it go and thought if they ever wanted to tell me what happened they would but they never did."

Mick's sister Rhonda (now Lucas) too felt somewhat neglected when her step siblings arrived although, she knew she was loved. Rhonda is five years older than Mick but she too has no vivid memory of her natural father.

"When Mick was born I was only five and we were living in a house at Port Arthur with my Mum and Nan but Dad was hardly ever home and I don't know why," Rhonda said.

"We had a good life even though we didn't have a Dad around to look after us. "

What led to Horace Burles and eldest son Robert leaving the family home and why Denis was adopted out remains a mystery to Rhonda as well.

"I would often ask Mum what happened to Robert and Denis and all she would say was, 'I don't know' and left it at that. We never worried too much about it because we were well cared for and didn't want for much," Rhonda said.

Despite having a relaxed lifestyle Rhonda says her mother didn't cope well with pressure.

"I think Mum had a tough life. She would often go all quiet and just sit there staring at nothing which is why Mick and I relied a lot on Nan if we had any issues that came along."

BEING estranged from his natural father meant Mick spent his formative years under the strict rule of his stepfather, a tough man who had little time for him or his sister.

"He didn't take too kindly to me from the outset and I remember vividly one day he chased me up the paddock trying to hit me with a bull whip but he couldn't catch me even though I was wearing size eight gumboots at the time—I was a nippy little bastard for a five- or six-year-old. He chased me because I'd called him an arsehole. Nan was a good judge of character and she never liked him from day one.

"Mum had four kids to my stepdad—Lynette, Sharon, Larry and Tim—and she gave most of her attention to those kids but we all got along. We never had much money but we still knew how to have fun and we had lots of it. I even grew to like my stepfather."

Time has a way of healing all wounds and this was clearly the case with Mick and his stepfather. Living in close quarters ensured that something had to give and thankfully for Mick he was able to make some sort of peace with Tony so they became a reasonably close-knit family unit. Mick still sees a lot of Lynette and Larry although he hardly ever sees Tim, while Sharon makes the odd appearance but has never made a point of staying in touch. Mick and his stepfather buried any misgivings they might have had for each other a long time ago. Tony remarried but now lives in an aged-care facility in Burnie on Tasmania's north-west coast.

"I have a lot of great memories growing up on the Peninsula and that includes spending a lot of time with my stepbrothers and sisters. My preschool years are a bit sketchy but overall I guess I was just like any other kid of my age who lived on a farm."

Most of Mick's closest friends were relatives, with his first cousins Frank Spaulding and David Nichols his best mates.

"Frank, David and me would go shooting and fishing a lot and two other kids who lived nearby, Dennis and Russell Rogers, pretty much made up our group. We were close mates and did heaps together and we all got up to no good at one stage or another but we never did anything that was against the law. Mum and Nan had drummed that into us from an early age."

Living on a farm meant Mick was responsible for daily chores before and after school and that included maintenance work around the house but he was always longing for a bush expedition. Spending time in the bush setting rabbit and wallaby snares and traps was his favourite pastime, although he also loved to spend a day fishing at Flat Rock, about a two-kilometre walk from the farmhouse to the foot of the 200-metre high cliffs that form the outline of the bottom end of Cape Raoul. This is some of the fiercest and most deadly waters surrounding the island state.

"We had the best fishing spot in the world pretty much on our back doorstep. We'd carry our rods and cray rings down to Flat Rock and we'd spend the day and night there. We'd come home with enough crayfish to last us a week and all sorts of fish. It was a brilliant spot because the fishing boats couldn't get in close to the cliffs because it was so rocky. Flat Rock was long and wide and set about 50 metres out from the cliff wall and it was a 30-fathom drop straight off the edge. You had to have your wits about you all the time because there was always a chance of a freak wave coming along. Only ever saw one and we were off the rock at the time—thank Christ."

Whatever Mick and his mates caught at Flat Rock was used for dinner and it was Mick's job also to clean and fillet the fish and keep the crays alive in make-shift saltwater tanks because there was no refrigerator in the Burles household.

"We never had a fridge so we had to divvy up whatever fish we caught and pretty much eat it that night but the crays were good for a week and I'd boil them and serve them up fresh every day."

Mick developed a strong work ethic from an early age with his day starting out rounding up the cows for early morning milking before heading off to school for a day of academic toil. His sister would also milk the cows before and after school. Mick knew he had to attend school but there was nothing in the rule book that said he had to like it.

"I didn't mind school on Fridays because that was sport day but I didn't go much on the reading, writing and arithmetic although I was no dummy. I passed all the subjects to go up a grade each year. I guess I was like all kids. I was more interested in spending my time shooting and fishing and playing sport than anything else.

"I was nearly six when I learned how to snare rabbits and I had my first smoke about the same age. It was my first day of school and before I headed down to the bus stop I'd sneak down to the local jetty and have a smoke I'd pinched out of Mum's packet. I don't know what made me want to have that cigarette but I wish I'd never had the bastard."

Mick was a regular churchgoer. His Mum and Nan would make sure he and Rhonda donned their best clothes every Sunday and the family would walk about two kilometres to the local church at Highcroft. Mick's uncle Hubert, his mother's brother, was the Minister and that gave Mick a few rights not gifted to many of the kids who had to sit through his sermons.

"I didn't mind going to church because that's where I learned to drink wine. Uncle Hubert had the wine out the back and he'd use it during the service but me and two of my mates used to sneak out back and get stuck into his 'holy nectar' as he called it and more often than not he'd have to fill up the chalice more than once during the service."

Farm life presented Mick with ample opportunities to be mischievous and playing pranks on his sister Rhonda was at the top of the list.

"I was a bugger of a kid really and some of the things I used to do to tease Rhonda, it's a wonder she still speaks to me. I used to grab her cat and take it up the bush and put it in a basket with the lid shut and go back to the house to see Rhonda crying because she couldn't find her cat. I'd just let her cry for a while and eventually I'd go and retrieve the cat and take it back to the house but only after Nan had given me a clip over the ears and a bit of a tongue lashing.

"One day we were playing in the paddock of one of our next-door neighbours' properties and hanging about the big frog pond and I thought it'd be hilarious if I pushed Rhonda into the pond so I did and when she went home crying she got a hiding from Nan for getting her clothes wet and muddy but Nan caught me laughing at her so she gave me a right old hiding too. I never pushed Rhonda in the pond again.

"My favourite thing was throwing stones at Rhonda on the way home from school and I'd tease her about anything I could. I can remember her having a heap of cuts and bruises on her arms and head from my accurate throws. I was a right prick of a kid really. But one day she retaliated and cracked me over the head with a hoe and by Christ it hurt so I laid off giving her a hard time for a while; but things eventually got back to normal."

When Mick wasn't giving his sister a tough time he was either playing sport or working the farm. It was Mick's responsibility to put some of the meat on the table.

"We would go out in the bush and set traps to catch the rabbits and wallabies and when I was older I'd take a gun and shoot the odd roo but we'd only ever get enough to feed the family."

Mick also found a way to earn some pocket money by selling pelts from the rabbits and wallabies to a fur trader who would visit the region from time to time.

"I never earned a hell of a lot from the rabbit and wallaby skins but it was enough to keep a jangle in my pocket."

Mick, his sister and four step-siblings were taught from a very young age to respect the fauna as a source of food and that the animals weren't to be used for target practice; this was also drummed into the children at school.

Although appreciative of the importance of being educated Mick would often try to wriggle out of school by faking an illness but his mother and Nan were too wise to be fooled by his poor acting skills.

Through adolescence Mick had a couple of mentors including next door neighbour Bill Bachelor who helped out with some old-fashioned tutoring.

"Bill Bachelor was a terrific old bloke. He helped teach me how to plough paddocks and ride horses and other farm stuff. He only had one eye. He lost one as a result of someone poking him with a stick when he was a kid. He was a funny old bastard but he had a bit of a soft spot for me and I used to love working with him around the farm.

"He used to like getting me riled up. One of his favourite pastimes was cracking the bull whip near the horse when I was ploughing and that made the horse go faster. I didn't go much on it but old Bill thought it was a great joke and would just sit back pissing himself laughing."

Mick became quite attached to the wily old farmer who one day gave everyone a scare when he failed to arrive home for dinner after he had been ploughing paddocks near the back boundary of his 80-hectare farm.

"Bill's missus came and asked me to look for Bill because he hadn't lobbed for his dinner and that was unusual for him because he loved his tucker. So I jumped on my horse and rode down to where he was supposed to be working and I saw the tractor on its side and when I got closer I saw that Bill's legs were pinned. It scared the shit out of me.

"I panicked and didn't even check to see if Bill was alive or dead. I just rode back to the house as quickly as I could to get help and his brother, who had the farm on the other side of us, drove his tractor down to where Bill was pinned and pulled the other tractor back on its wheels and Bill walked away pretty much unharmed."

"He just had a bit of a limp for a few days. He was a tough old bastard because he was back working the tractor the next day."

Unbeknown to Mick it was Bill Bachelor's work ethic and sense of humour that would have an everlasting effect on his life.

ALTHOUGH Mick resented the need to attend school, one subject that never held him back was maths. English troubled him as did a few of the other staples including history and geography but his love of maths was probably a result of regular trips to his Nan's wardrobe where he and his sister would rifle through her famous money tins.

"Nan used to collect biscuit tins and that's where she used to hide her money. Every time Nan got a pension cheque she'd get it cashed and roll up some of the cash, put a rubber band around it and load the roll into the tin. Me and Rhonda would wait until she was out of the house and raid the wardrobe and count all the money. There were rolls of anywhere between £20 and £30 and we'd unravel them and count it out; there was heaps there.

"There were five or six of these big biscuit tins and they were just full of money. We'd never want to pinch any, we just wanted to count it. We didn't really know what money was all about back then. Nan would catch us counting it so she'd growl at us and we'd just roll it all up again and put the tins back in the wardrobe. I reckon Nan didn't have a problem with us getting to the biscuit tins because she knew it was teaching us how to count and the more we did it the better we got at counting."

Sissy Nichols knew how to live off the land but she also had a good head on her shoulders for business. She knew how to save and it was her ability to hide part or all of her pension money each month that provided enough to buy the farm at Stormlea from which the entire family was able to derive a living. When Sissy died of a heart attack in 1963, Mick was on Maria Island with his scout group.

"We'd gone on a scout camp for three days and left on a Friday so Nan must have died that night but I wasn't told she'd passed away until I got home the following Monday. I knew there was something wrong when I overheard Mum telling the scout master, who also was the school head master, that I wouldn't be going to school all that week."

Losing his Nan was a bitter blow to Mick. "Nan was everything to me and Rhonda because Mum only had eyes for my stepfather and the kids they produced. I suppose I never realised how much I loved Nan until she died."

SISSY Nichols left the farm to Rhonda and Mick with their mother and the children's step-father left out of the will.

It took two years for the farm to sell and once finalised Rhonda and Mick were to each receive £600 from the sale. Mick was almost 17 when the sale was finalised and he was quick off the mark to withdraw his money while Rhonda kept hers at the bank but it was in her and her mother's name.

"Mum kept saying she needed money for this and that and my stepdad would go to the bank and withdraw whatever Mum had asked for but when I went to withdraw my money there wasn't a lot left. I kept myself with what was left in the bank but I made sure that Mum and Tony couldn't access my account when I started work."

Rhonda's first job was at the Four Seasons Motel at Port Arthur where she worked as a house maid and later as a waitress. She saved what money she could because her plan was to eventually have enough money to set up a place of her own and hopefully meet the man of her dreams.

Before the family decided to relocate to Burnie on the north-west coast Rhonda met Ross Lucas at the Port Arthur pub and a solid relationship was spawned following their first date on her 21st birthday.

"I met Ross at my 21st party that we held at the local pub. It was pretty much love at first sight for me and after that I had no eyes for any other man."

Rhonda stayed with the family when they relocated to Burnie not long after but as soon as she was able and had enough money saved, she returned to Port Arthur to marry her first love and they produced three children Trudy, Gavin and Craig. Ross worked for the Department of Forestry and Rhonda was quick to adapt to living in dense rural settings.

"The first house we lived in as a couple was at Branxholm (north-east of Launceston) and that was on a normal building block but we were only there for a couple of years because it was normal for forestry workers to move from place to place and Ross was one of the supervisors so we were moved about more than most. We moved to a place at Springfield near Scottsdale but then Ross was transferred to Ouse in the Derwent Valley and that was terrible because it was so isolated."

"But I guess the main reason I hated Ouse was because it was while we were there Ross met another woman and our marriage collapsed. I moved out with the kids and we went to live in Launceston and he lived with his new girlfriend. It was a terrible time in my life and for the children but we got through it.

"Had it not been for Ross's parents, Ellen and Bob Lucas, I would have found it very difficult to survive. Although they didn't help out financially it was the friendship they offered that helped ease the pain of having to live a life as a single mother. My mother-in-law (Ellen) became my closest friend." Making her way as a single mother living off a sole parent pension made life tough for her and the children.

"I received about $80 a month from Ross so the pension was pretty much all we could live on while the kids were at school but we managed somehow and the kids never went without much."

Rhonda never remarried, preferring to concentrate on raising her children with the help of her in-laws.

"Once my relationship with Ross ended I pretty much decided never to remarry. There were times when I thought it would be good for the kids to have a father figure as a constant in their lives but they still got to see their natural father from time to time and their Pop (Bob Lucas) was a good substitute."

Rhonda lives in an aged-care facility in Launceston and keeps in regular contact with her children and Mick gets at least one phone call a month from his big sister who constantly reminds him how much better his life would have been had he not been a smoker.

2

Way up North

BY the age of 17 Mick Burles considered himself quite the lady's man, so much so he used to have bets with his mates that he could, in his terms, "latch onto a sheila and bed her within hours of meeting her".

Although that is wrong on so many levels by today's standards it wasn't so when Mick, in a flashy sports shirt, stove-pipe jeans and winkle pickers (pointy toed shoes), drove through the streets of Port Arthur with streamers and a fox tail billowing on the tip of the souped-up VC Valiant's car radio aerial like a windsock at the local airstrip.

These were the 1960s and Mick was doing as he pleased with not a care in the world. It was a time when Elvis Presley was a waning heartthrob of most female teenagers in Australia and when The Beatles were taking the world by storm. Armed with a few fancy dance moves and a bevy of proven one-liners, Mick spent a fair amount of time doing what all healthy teenage boys did when they went to dances or the local pub on a Friday or Saturday night.

Mick would find a girl in the crowd and then bet his mates that he could walk out of the pub with her attached to his arm within five minutes of introducing himself to her.

"There was this one night at the local pub at Port Arthur that proved quite profitable, in more ways than one. There were three girls sitting across the other side of the bar and I bet my mates I could have one of the girls leave the pub with me within five minutes. The money was on so I strolled over and asked if I could buy them all a drink. I got the drinks and when I delivered one to this girl in a white dress I accidentally—on purpose—spilt the drink all over her. I apologised and offered to take her home to get changed so we left the pub inside five minutes."

"I took her home to her place and she got changed but we didn't get back to the pub until two hours later after getting sidetracked. I collected my money from the boys and ended up taking a different sheila home that night."

Mick's sweet talking charm eventually led him to a year-long trip to Queensland. "I met these four girls who had been picking apples in the region and they wanted to go to Queensland to pick oranges and mandarins and that sounded like a good idea so I booked the car on the old Princess of Tasmania and off we went. There was a German, an Italian, a Frenchie and a Pom. They all spoke with broad accents.

"I'd become friends with a bloke who'd been fruit picking and he wanted a lift back to Queensland so he joined the crew for the trip north."

Mick was cashed up after his inheritance and that, coupled with a sizeable amount he'd been able to save along the way from his job as an apprentice chef, selling rabbit and wallaby pelts, fruit picking and other odd jobs, he had been able to pay cash for his new Valiant as well as buying new threads and still having ample cash reserves to ensure his adventure to Queensland would be an enjoyable one.

He had only just acquired his driver's licence but as he'd been driving tractors since he was 10, driving held no fears for this cocky teenager.

"All I could think about was getting out of Tasmania to explore some of the places I'd heard so much about and to be doing it with four gorgeous sheilas was too good an opportunity to pass up."

The Valiant had a leather lay-back front bench seat and was built for comfort but six in a car built to accommodate five was always going to be cramped. The trip across Bass Strait went smoothly and it gave Mick time to really get to know a couple of his travelling companions. The journey to Queensland took two weeks with Mick mapping out a route that took them first to Mount Buller, a popular ski resort in the Alpine region of Victoria, about three hours drive from Melbourne.

"I'd been to Mount Wellington in Hobart to see the snow but it was nothing compared to what I saw at Buller. It was just this sea of snow and it was every bit as good as I'd been told it would be and the girls loved it too. There was probably a bit of method in my madness heading to Mount Buller because there is a best way to keep warm on cold nights and I had plans to keep as warm as I could. Needless to say I had the best nights ever."

The group then headed north to Canberra and Sydney, staying in backpacker hostels along the way. "I wanted the trip to drag out as long as I could because I wanted to give myself as much time as possible to really get to know the girls. The girls were fun-loving types and we all got on well."

The ultimate destination was Mundubbera, a small town about 400 kilometres north-west of Brisbane. Mundubbera is the self-proclaimed citrus capital of Queensland, although that has always been the subject of protest from the neighbouring town of Gayndah. The orchard Mick targeted was The Golden Mile. "When we got to Mundubbera it felt something like home. I don't know what it was about the place but I somehow felt safe and content."

Mick and the girls spent about three months working in various orchards but he soon grew tired of that when the girls moved on. Mick looked for different employment in the town and it was his ability to work a farm that paid dividends.

"I used to go to the local pharmacy and got to know the owner's two daughters who worked there and when I told them I needed to find some work and that I could drive a tractor their Dad offered me work on one of three farms that he owned."

Mick loved working the farm but his elevated libido again caused him some grief. "One of the daughters would bring me what she called my midnight lunch most nights. I'd get on the tractor and she'd straddle the seat facing me and we'd do a few laps of the paddock and that went on for quite a while. But her old man got wind of it and sent me out to another one of his farms way out in the sticks and there was no action there. All of a sudden living in Mundubbera wasn't so shit hot."

Mick was also involved in a car accident while in Mundubbera and was lucky to escape unscathed. "Im not sure where we were heading but I was in the back seat and in the front were the driver, a woman who was about eight months' pregnant in the middle and another bloke in the passenger seat. The car launched into the air and crashed into a bridge and ended up on its roof as flat as a pancake, but nobody was badly injured."

"There were no seat belts, so those in the front were thrown from the car on impact and I was ejected when the nose of the car hit the ground so it was empty when if flipped onto its roof. They found me about 20 metres further down the road with a deep gash in my head but the pregnant girl never had a scratch on her and the two blokes also got away with some scratches and bruises. We were all lucky to be alive. I spent over a week in hospital but there were no broken bones—just the head wounds and I had a pretty bad concussion"

But the accident only prevented Mick from working for a couple of weeks and he knew he had to get back to it because it was now the only money he had to live on. He also was keen to get back to playing football.

Mick loved his footy (Aussie Rules) so while still living at Mundubbera he ventured down to Brisbane in the pre-season for a couple of practice matches with the Morningside Football Club.

"I thought it would be a good idea to get involved with a footy club because I missed playing the game. I'd heard of Morningside so I made a beeline for that club and found the blokes to be good fellas so I signed up."

With the girls gone and no other reason to stick around Mundubbera he packed his bags, jumped in the Valiant and headed to Brisbane where he quickly scored a job in a furniture factory, just before the start of the footy season.

"I wasn't too impressed with working in a factory, processing orders for dispatch, but it was a job and it gave me an income and allowed me to play footy," he said.

Mick was a talented footballer and while he was never going to make it in a major league he was an asset to any team in the local Brisbane competition and he more than held his own at Morningside. However when Morningside failed to make the finals he said his goodbye to teammates, paid his respects to a couple of female acquaintances and headed back to Tasmania.

3

Back Home

WHEN the ship docked at Devonport on a glorious spring morning in September 1968, Mick was unsure what lay ahead but he knew he needed a family fix and set about finding out where his mother and stepfather were living in Burnie on the state's north-west coast. He had no idea what to expect when he landed on their doorstep.

Mick had stayed in touch with his Mum while he was gallivanting around Queensland so with her phone number at the ready he pounced on the first public phone box he could find and made the call. Mick scribbled 8 Payne Street onto a piece of paper he'd ripped out of the phone book and made a beeline for what would be his new place of abode.

"I knew Mum and the family had moved to Burnie so I made the call and lobbed on their doorstep. It felt good to be home but in a way I was sad because as the boat was crossing Bass Strait I couldn't help but feel a sense of finality about what I'd been doing for the past 18 months and thought about where I might head for my next adventure. I didn't know whether I was going to be able to settle back into the lifestyle I had before I went to Queensland."

With little money left he immediately sought work and landed a job at the local sawmill.

"The job at the sawmill wasn't much but it was enough to get me a wage each week so I could pay my way. Living at home again was good and while it was a bit cramped for room Mum made a fuss and that made me feel good and Tony was still the same but we were getting along better in those days. Although I upset him a bit when he complained about having to walk up a passage to get from the kitchen to the lounge room so I went out the back, grabbed a chain saw and cut a hole in the dividing wall in the shape of a doorway.

"I was a stupid bastard because I never checked for electrical wiring or anything like that. I smirked at Tony and told him he should be happy because he wouldn't have to walk down the passage any more and he just laughed at me and went and got another beer."

Mick easily fell back into the Tasmanian lifestyle and one thing that hadn't changed while he was away was the night life.

"It didn't take me long to find out where all the top sheilas gathered on a Friday and Saturday night so that was one good thing about being home.

"I thought I'd make the most of whatever came along because at the back of my mind I kept thinking about some of the places that I might go to next but I wasn't in any rush. I was 19, and had not a care in the world."

He was also looking forward to playing football again because he thought he'd become a better player having had the experience with Morningside in the top Brisbane competition.

But as he'd arrived back home at the end of winter he made it known around town that he was keen to play cricket and the offers poured in. From his first pay packet he bought cricket whites and a pair of cricket boots but he relied on the club to provide all the accessories such as bats, gloves, pads and the box that would protect the crown jewels.

He joined the Ridgley Cricket Club, a member of the North-West Coast Regional Cricket Association and after a few practice sessions in the nets he was quickly identified as a handy medium-fast bowler. In the opening game against Sassafras he was handed the new ball.

"I wasn't what you would call an express fast bowler but I bowled right-arm over the wicket and made the batsmen earn every run; at least that was the aim. I took my fair share of wickets and I can only remember being given a caning once that season and it was a bloke who made a stack of runs and a lot of them came from two or three of my overs.

"I'd never seen that sort of hitting before. I at least had the pleasure of running him out when he was going for a sharp single. The poor bastard was on 99 when he hit a drive straight to me at cover and picked it up clean and threw the pill as straight as a dye to hit the middle stump at the bowler's end and he was short of his crease by a mile.

Mick ended the season without having made an impact on the scoreboard with the bat but he'd done his job with the ball.

4

In the Army

JUST when Mick was starting to make an impact on the Burnie nightlife, he was drafted into the Army. He warmed to the idea quickly and decided to treat it as his next adventure.

He was still 19 but as his birthday fell between April 1 and June 30 he was included in the 1969 intake. The National Archives tell the story:

> *"The National Service Act, passed on 24 November 1964, required 20 year-old males, if selected, to serve in the Army for a period of two years of continuous service (later reduced to eighteen months in 1971), followed by three years in the Reserve. The Defence Act was amended in May 1965 to provide that conscripts could be obliged to serve overseas, and in March 1966, Prime Minister Harold Holt announced that National Servicemen would be sent to Vietnam to fight in units of the Australian Regular Army."*
>
> *Between 1965 and December 1972 more than 800,000 Australian men registered for National Service. About 63,000 were conscripted and more than 19,000 served in Vietnam.*

Although registration was compulsory a process of selection by ballot determined who would be called up. Two ballots were conducted each year. The ballots selected several dates in the selected period and all males with corresponding birthdays were called up for national service. The ballot was conducted using a lottery barrel and marbles representing birthdays. The original barrel and marbles that were used in the process are held in the National Office, Canberra.[1]

"The thought of what Army life might offer was quite appealing," Mick said, "so I ended up quite excited about the prospects of learning something new and maybe get the chance to help defend my country."

Once he passed all the medical examinations, in March 1969 Mick was off to the Army training camp at Puckapunyal in Victoria, not far from the town of Seymour, 90 kilometres north of Melbourne on the Hume Highway.

Army training posed no problems for Mick who was already a crack shot with a rifle having spent his early years honing his skills on the Tasman Peninsula. With only still targets as the objectives at shooting practice Mick was quickly recognised as a potential marksman.

"Once I'd finished with the first three months of basic training I loved being in the Army because I was good with a rifle and everything else we had to do to successfully complete our basic training. Once I'd come to terms with taking orders everything was sweet.

"When the officers worked out that a bloke could shoot they pissed him off out of it and concentrated on the ones who couldn't do it and they even got us blokes who were good shots to help teach the others. It was either that or we'd be sent back to camp to polish our boots or some other mundane job just to give us something to do."

At the end of training Mick fully expected to eventually get a posting that might lead him to serve in Vietnam. He wasn't afraid of going overseas because he was keen to put all the training to good use. At the

1 Source: National Archives of Australia (naa.gov.au)

end of basic training the recruits all participated in the official march out parade and then headed to which ever corps they had been assigned and Mick was elated to have been attached to the infantry.

"I was hanging out for corps training because that's when we'd be spending a lot more time out in the bush and I was really looking forward to that. We were all looking forward to going to Singleton."

The Australian Army School of Infantry is located at Singleton, about 200 kilometres north-west of Sydney and about 80 kilometres north-west of Newcastle. The population of Singleton is 14,000 but would have been significantly higher between 1960 and 1980.

Singleton Training Camp is where all infantry training was carried out during the National Service era.

"When we arrived at Singleton I felt right at home. The corps training involved learning to do things that are required in combat situations. Things such as section work, how to read maps and sign language that is required when on patrol in a war zone. It was all interesting stuff and I was starting to feel a part of something special. Some of the stuff came naturally but other stuff was hard to take in but we all got it right eventually. I remember the full pack drill was to run 20 kilometres carrying a full pack on your back. At the end of the run the rifle felt like it weighed as much as a bloody cannon. It was hard yakka but it's what we needed to get ready for going overseas to fight."

Again Mick was singled out for his brilliance with a rifle. It had him thinking of becoming a sniper with a trip to Vietnam almost assured. Mick was disappointed when his commanding officer gave him the news that he wouldn't be going to Vietnam but instead he would be sent back at Puckapunyal as an instructor to train recruits on how to use a rifle.

"Initially I was pissed off when they told me I'd have to go back to Pucka but I didn't feel as bad a few months later. A lot of the blokes in my regiment who did get posted to Vietnam at the same time I would have been due to go came home with all sorts of problems and injuries. A couple of them didn't come home.

"There was one bloke in our regiment, Parsissons was his surname but we all just knew him as Pa, went to Vietnam and got his leg blown up pretty bad when he trod on a mine. About 200 stitches were needed to put his leg back together and after a couple of months he went back, stood on another mine and that stuffed him completely."

From the time of the arrival of the first batch of Australian troops sent to Vietnam in 1962 almost 60,000 Australians, including ground troops, air force and navy personnel, served in the region. 521 died as a result of the war and more than 3,000 were wounded.

"A lot of the blokes I served with who went to Vietnam came back with all sorts of mental and health issues and what hurt most was that those who did serve over there were treated shabbily. They got little or no recognition. All they were doing was fighting for their country. I still carry that little bit of regret that I didn't go to Vietnam but when I reflect back on what that war did to so many Australians I should probably thank my lucky stars that they sent me back to Puckapunyal."

The Army also gave Mick the chance to finish off an apprenticeship he started when he was a teenager. When he made it known that he could cook he was encouraged to prepare meals at the officers' mess at night. That gig lasted just over a year. Although Mick was unable to secure a chef's ticket from the experience, he learned enough to consider carving a carer from cooking once he had finished National Service.

During daylight Mick was teaching new recruits to become proficient riflemen but he also focused on staying fit. Outside of the regular 20-kilometre training runs he found other ways to improve his fitness. His love of Aussie Rules meant playing for the Army Infantry against other corps as well as combined teams against the Navy and Air Force, so footy practice and playing friendly games were at least something he had to look forward to in the winter months. He also was given the opportunity to play with and against some of the best from the (then) Victorian Football League.

Some of the highest profile players to ever don a footy jumper were engaged in National Service during Mick's time, and North Melbourne was seeking a decent pre-season practice match and decided to pit itself against a team made up of National Service draftees. In 1970 the Army team boasted some high-profile players including Kevin Sheedy and Rex Hunt. With such depth of talent running around Puckapunyal at the time it wasn't hard to put together a team that might give any VFL team a run for its money in a practice match.

"The football match was the talk of Seymour and us Army blokes were real keen to have a crack because we had some of the best players from all over Australia doing National Service at the time. The opposition fielded a few experienced players along with some young ones who they wanted to have a good look at.

"I got picked to play because I was from Tassie and I'd been able to show what I could do in a couple of practice matches we had before the big game and we were all probably as fit as we've ever been in our lives because of all the training we'd been doing.

"I started out on a wing and had a few touches but when our full-forward had to come off with an injury I was asked to moved to full-forward. When I took up my position Sam Kekovich was playing full-back and he was a mean, tough son of a bitch."

Sam Kekovich played 124 games with North Melbourne from 1968 to 1976 and he won the club's best and fairest award in his second year with the club. But in more recent times Kekovich has gained fame (or infamy, depending on your point of view!) for his performances in television commercials as ambassador (or self-proclaimed 'ambassador) for the Australian lamb Industry. Kekovich's flatly delivered satirical monologues delight in using wide-ranging cultural references, contrasting many incongruous images and ideas. At the end comes Sam's trademark: 'You know it makes sense. I'm Sam Kekovich.' Mick recalls the game like it was yesterday: "I was surprised Kekovich was put at full-back because he had made his mark on the game as a forward. Anyhow it didn't bother me because Kekovich wasn't the fastest mover and I was a nippy little bastard.

I had a good leap and could kick the ball a long way. In no time I've kicked three goals and was cocky enough to let Kekovich know about it.

"I was rapt because the move had paid off but the next thing I know Kekovich is in my ear telling me to enjoy what I'd just done because I wouldn't be kicking any more goals. No sooner had he said that I've sped off on a lead and about to take what was going to be an easy chest mark when crunch! I felt this horrible pain at the back of my neck like I'd been hit with a pick-axe and down I went.

"I woke up in the change rooms. I told him over a beer later on that I'd get him back one day but I never did."

Mick served out his two years without playing another game against such a star-studded team but that one game established a bond between him and Kekovich; they would often catch up at race meetings in Victoria as Kekovich was an avid racing fan. Kekovich remembers the match well, and in typical Keka style he said: "I'd say the only reason Burlsy has been so successful as a horse trainer is because I probably knocked some sense into him."

The Army had become an integral part of Mick's life so it was no chore for him to enlist with the Tasmanian Army Reserve which was compulsory for any recruit who did not serve overseas or who didn't want to join the regular Army by the time his two-year stint of National Service had expired.

"I loved Army life but I couldn't go as far as making it a career so when I arrived back in Tassie I enlisted in the Army Reserve. I was in the Reserve for about nine years, which was way more than you were required to do.

"It was one night a week at the barracks or the rifle range and we'd go away for two weeks every year on bivouac. Because I was such a crack shot with a rifle I continued to teach blokes how to shoot and I loved that. The Reserve gave me a break from normal life. I think most of the fellas in my battalion were in the same boat."

When Mick returned home from National Service he had a job waiting for him at the Burnie Paper Mill so it was just a matter of selecting where at the Mill he wanted to work.

Anyone who had committed to two years National Service had the guarantee of a job at their place of work before they had been called up. Once a job was locked away, Mick set about hooking up with a football club armed with the added experience he had gained in the Army. He was as fit as he'd ever been in his life and the stringy midfielder-forward was taken on by the Penguin Football Club, then a dominant force in the North-West Tasmanian Football League (NWTFL).

Mick was never going to be a star at the game but those who played with him say he had good ability but most importantly he was courageous, quick and was an accurate kick, three of the key ingredients needed to play the game well.

Mick continued to play football right up until he was 44. He says his tally of matches played is 494 but he also coached more than 300 games, many as a playing coach.

"I rarely missed a season of footy right up until I had to give it away in 1993. That was a hard pill to swallow because I only needed six more games to crack the 500 mark but my back was so bad I couldn't take the chance of copping a tackle that could have put me in a wheelchair for life. In the end 494 wasn't a bad effort."

Mick's tally of games covered the whole state. He played with Port Arthur in the Tasman League until he was 17 and after returning from Queensland he had a plethora of clubs from which to choose. He played for Burnie reserves after a stint in the under-19s but he was unable to break into the senior side.

"Burnie had a top senior list when I was there so I had no problems with playing in the reserves because at least I was getting a game and it was a really good club to be a part of back then. In fact they say it's still one of the great football clubs in Tasmania."

Mick played with Penguin for a few years before playing a season or two with Cuprona, Ridgley and Yeoman and when he relocated to Deloraine he signed on with the Red Hills Football Club and he remembers one game in particular against Meander that left a clear imprint of how tough the game can be played.

"The Red Hills boys were pretty tough and I was right at home with 'em but one day against Meander there was a bit of a dust-up on our forward line just as the final siren sounded. I wasn't involved but when one of our blokes hit the deck and was knocked out cold we all just rushed in and next thing it's turned into an all-in brawl. There were bodies laid out all over the ground and that included supporters from both sides."

Mick ended up playing in the Northern Districts Amateur League when he moved to Georgetown, where he played and coached. When he relocated to Longford he continued in amateur competition where he ended his playing days. When he coached the South Launceston Under 19s to a Grand Final in 1999 he had ended his involvement with a sport that had been a constant in his life for almost four decades.

5

Falling in Love

WHEN Mick returned home from the Army he was again a 'freeagent' only because the girl he had been seeing regularly before his time in the Army, had fallen for a new bloke, from Woolnorth on the far north-west tip of the state.

Mick took to sawmill duties easily but when one of his workmates suggested he might be better off moving from the sawmill to another section of the business known as Paper Makers, he was curious.

Paper Makers had more than 100 women working in the factory, so he thought that was right up his alley. Needless to say Mick applied to be transferred and as a returned serviceman he got what he wanted. He was only a week into the new job when he caught the eye of one of the girls on the floor, who also had taken a shine to him—from a distance. Lynnette Groves was a 20-year-old dark-haired beauty who was born and raised in Burnie and she loomed as a nice catch should Mick be able to woo her.

"I'd been watching this sheila for a while. The whites of her eyes were like beacons and I'd never seen any woman with eyes like that before. She was real pretty so she pretty much ticked all the boxes as far as I was concerned. But I was a bit afraid of asking her out on a date because I was worried she'd knock me back and I wasn't big on rejection—never have been.

"But it seemed like every time I looked at her she was perving on me too. One day I was talking to one of my workmates about whether or not the sheila with the big eyes would be worth a shot and bugger me dead if her sister Jodi wasn't standing near me when we were yakking about her. Next thing Jodi pipes up and says, 'why don't you ask her out 'cause I reckon she'd say yes'."

Mick, armed with this useful intel, plucked up the courage to introduce himself and he was more than pleased when she responded with a yes.

"I'd never been so worried about asking a girl out in my life. I had butterflies in the stomach when I was trying to ask her out but when she agreed I then had to think quickly and come up with a decent place to take her out to dinner.

"My mates had told me about this ripper joint in Ulverstone that had good tucker and it wasn't too expensive so that's where we went. After dinner we went to a drive-in (movie) but I'm buggered if I can remember what the movie was because we just talked most of the time.

"When I look back on that first night there's no doubt that I fell in love for the one and only time in my life. Lynn was a good looker, she had a great sense of humour and that suited me right down to the ground. She didn't mind a drink and like me she smoked; what more could a bloke ask for in a woman? But the one thing that stuck with me after that first date was that I never thought of getting her into bed once during the whole night. I gave her a kiss when I dropped her home and I pretty much knew I was hooked."

The courtship lasted a year and when Mick finally proposed they were both ready to start a new life together. Together they had enjoyed a great social life and six months into the relationship they had even started up a joint bank account, which was new territory for Mick. Until then he had become astute at spending everything he earned from pay to pay.

The relationship had grown both spiritually and physically although the first time Mick and Lyn were intimate it was under very strange circumstances. Mick says it was a short but sweet encounter on the porch where Mick would always kiss his girl goodnight at her parents' home. The four Groves girls lived under a strict regime with Lyn's father Jack imposing curfews on week nights and Sundays for all the girls while they lived under his roof.

"If Jack had ever found out what we got up to on the porch just inside the front door that night, I reckon he would have killed me. It was just so spontaneous. Neither of us had ever tried to do anything like that before, least of all in her home. Many years later we would talk about it and have a good laugh."

Mick Burles and Lynette Groves were married at the Baptist Church in Burnie in April 1972, almost a year to the day after their first date. The bride's parents Jack and Molly Groves dipped into their savings to give another one of their daughters a white wedding. The Groves had four girls, Sandra, Jodi, Lyn and Peta but it was Lyn who held the trump card to her father's heart.

The invitation list for Mick and Lyn's wedding was huge with more than 150 guests attending the service and reception, of which 90 were Mick's family and friends. Mick even sent invitations to his estranged brothers Robert and Denis but he was not surprised when neither attended.

"I sent invites to my brothers but they were sent to their last known addresses so maybe they didn't ever get them or maybe they did and just couldn't be bothered. Anyway I did my bit and them not being there didn't worry me."

Mick's closest footy mates filled a pew in the church and, according to Mick, when toasts to the groom were made at the reception that night most of the raucous comments came from the footy crew.

Mick and Lyn began married life together in a quaint little two-bedroom rented house at 12 Lucas Place in Burnie and it was there that they spent their first year together. Only two months into the marriage Lyn fell pregnant.

The joyous occasion was celebrated the night Lyn received the good news from her local GP and Mick was quick to organise a piss-up at the local to tell all and sundry he was about to become a Dad. But Lyn's father put a dampener on things when he turned his nose up at the news believing that his daughter had misled the family, convinced the child had been conceived out of wedlock.

Jack Groves was a Freemason who first joined the Masonic Lodge in 1961. He worked his way up the pecking order holding the position of worship master on four separate occasions with the Burnie Lodge from 1970 to 1989. When he died in April 1995 he was a life member of the Grand Lodge and had been issued with the Order of Distinction by the Tasmanian Grand Lodge, an honour that is not easily attained in the fraternity. He was a senior warden with the Burnie Grand Lodge, a position earned partly because of his moral views and standing in the community. Should what he believed to be true about his daughter ever reached the town's gossipmongers it could have had grave repercussions at the Lodge.

"Jack was a grumpy old bastard and he never spoke to Lyn all the way through her pregnancy because he was convinced she was up the duff before we got married. But when Kim arrived 11 months after the wedding he realised he'd made a blue and started talking to her again but he never apologised and I thought that was bad form," said Mick.

But Mick and Lyn never made too much of a fuss about her father's interpretation because Lyn's parents made a real fuss of their new grandson. About a year after Kim arrived Mick and Lyn set about saving to buy a house and when they had enough for a deposit they settled on a run-down three-bedroom weatherboard in Penguin. They both agreed it would be a great investment. By this time second son Damian had arrived, and the extra mouth to feed slowed the savings train. Lyn was the one who kept the bank balance growing as Mick had begun tinkering with the punt at the local TAB in what was rapidly becoming something of a ritual before he set off to play football. Little did he know that his few casual each way bets and daily doubles in Melbourne and Sydney would eventually lead to far more extravagant dealings with the Totalisator Agency Board.

Buying a house was special for Mick because he had always been told by his Nan that owning property was the best investment anyone can make. "Our first house at Penguin wasn't much to look at but at least it was ours and I knew that I could do a lot of work myself and turn it into a really nice place and that's what we did. Lyn was great at making a home and I was pretty handy with the tools, so after a few renovations and a spruce up inside, we had ourselves a nice place. The extensions I had planned had to be sped up when our daughter Carissa was born."

Life had panned out just as Mick had hoped. He'd married the best looking girl in town and she had presented him with three children. Lyn referred to the kids as gifts from God. If Mick believed that life was like a game of cards then he had been surely dealt a full hand when he married Lyn. The first five years of married life was wonderful for the couple with Mick working hard to make sure his young family had everything they needed and while their existence was far from extravagant, they wanted for little and were content with their lot.

Weekend camping trips were a constant in their lives although with Mick still in the Army Reserve he often had to reshuffle the family outings to accommodate monthly bivouacs. The arrival of Carissa gave Mick more responsibility but that never worried him, although just before her arrival it did cost him a trip to Hawaii with the Army.

"I had always wanted to go to Hawaii and the 12th Battalion was set to head to Hawaii for a week and I was really looking forward to it but when the dates came through for the trip I had to knock it back because it was right at the time Lyn was due to have our third child.

"But when Carissa came along it was a magical moment and I couldn't give a stuff about missing the trip to Hawaii. I loved the boys but it's just a different feeling that a father has for his daughter. Although I must admit it seemed that every time I took my belt off Lyn got pregnant so soon after Carissa was born I suggested to Lyn that we might shut up shop for a while. She agreed even though she would have been just as happy to keep pumping them out."

With the family unit growing and with Lyn keen to have more children Mick was starting to get itchy feet with his job at the mill. The long hours and shift work were starting to wear him down. He had spent much of his spare time working on renovations to the house and as they neared completion he convinced Lyn it might be time to sell and upgrade. But as they made plans to put the house on the market Mick felt it was also time for a career change.

Not long after Mick and Lyn had a binding contract of sale on their house at Penguin Mick decided to give up his job at Paper Makers and become a share-farmer. Although he had never been actively engaged in the profession he was sure it would be a lifestyle he could handle, having been raised on a farm, but it also was a job and lifestyle that would be appreciated by his young wife who was committed to being a full-time mum with three youngsters clamouring around her feet.

Mick had been making noises about share-farming to some of the dairy farmers on the north-west coast but the inquiries fell on deaf ears. Then he came across an advertisement in the local newspaper placed by prominent Central Districts dairy farmer Tony Wadley, who was looking for a share-farmer—preferably someone with a dairy farming background.

"When I saw the ad in the paper all of a sudden I could see everything falling into place. Wadley had a decent sized farm at Moltema near Deloraine with a herd of about 120 cows and he also grew crops like kale and oats. It was ideal and while there was no house with the deal there was a nice three-bedroom brick home available just 10 minutes from the farm."

Within a week of shaking hands on the deal Mick and his family were

Mick's Grandmother Sissy Nichols was a great influence on Mick's upbringing. She is pictured here (left), with Mick's mother Valerie (right), Mick (front centre) with his sister Rhonda (middle back) and his step-sister Lynette. (PHOTO: MICK BURLES PERSONAL COLLECTION)

Mick grew up with his four step-siblings and he is pictured with them, Lynette (back), front (L-R) Larry, Sharon and Tim. (PHOTO: MICK BURLES PERSONAL COLLECTION)

Mick was drafted into the Army in 1970 and he is pictured here (second row seated-six from left with the hat well and truly slouched!) with S Platoon at Puckapunyal.

(PHOTO: MICK BURLES PERSONAL COLLECTION)

Mick was a family man and he is pictured here with his wife Lyn who is holding their youngest son Dion with (front L-R) Damien, Carissa and Kim.
(PHOTO: MICK BURLES PERSONAL COLLECTION)

Mick was a crack marksman in the Army and he is pictured here with fellow rifleman Max Garcia as they pose for a photograph during an Army Reserve recruitment drive.
(PHOTO: MICK BURLES PERSONAL COLLECTION)

Mick took time out from Army duties to attend his sister Rhonda's wedding.
(PHOTO: MICK BURLES PERSONAL COLLECTION)

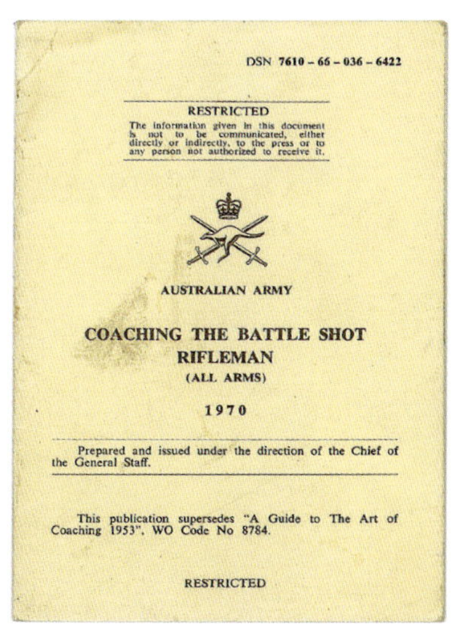

DSN 7610 – 66 – 036 – 6422

RESTRICTED

The information given in this document is not to be communicated, either directly or indirectly, to the press or to any person not authorized to receive it.

AUSTRALIAN ARMY

COACHING THE BATTLE SHOT RIFLEMAN

(ALL ARMS)

1970

Prepared and issued under the direction of the Chief of the General Staff.

This publication supersedes "A Guide to The Art of Coaching 1953", WO Code No 8784.

RESTRICTED

During his service Mick was an instructor with the Army Reserve and he always had his manual at the ready.
(PHOTO: MICK BURLES PERSONAL COLLECTION)

Mick gives the thumbs up after one of The Cleaner's wins in Hobart.
(PHOTO: MICK BURLES PERSONAL COLLECTION)

Trackwork rider David Quinn puts The Cleaner through his paces around the back roads of Longford in preparation for the 2015 Cox Plate.
(PHOTO: MICK BURLES PERSONAL COLLECTION)

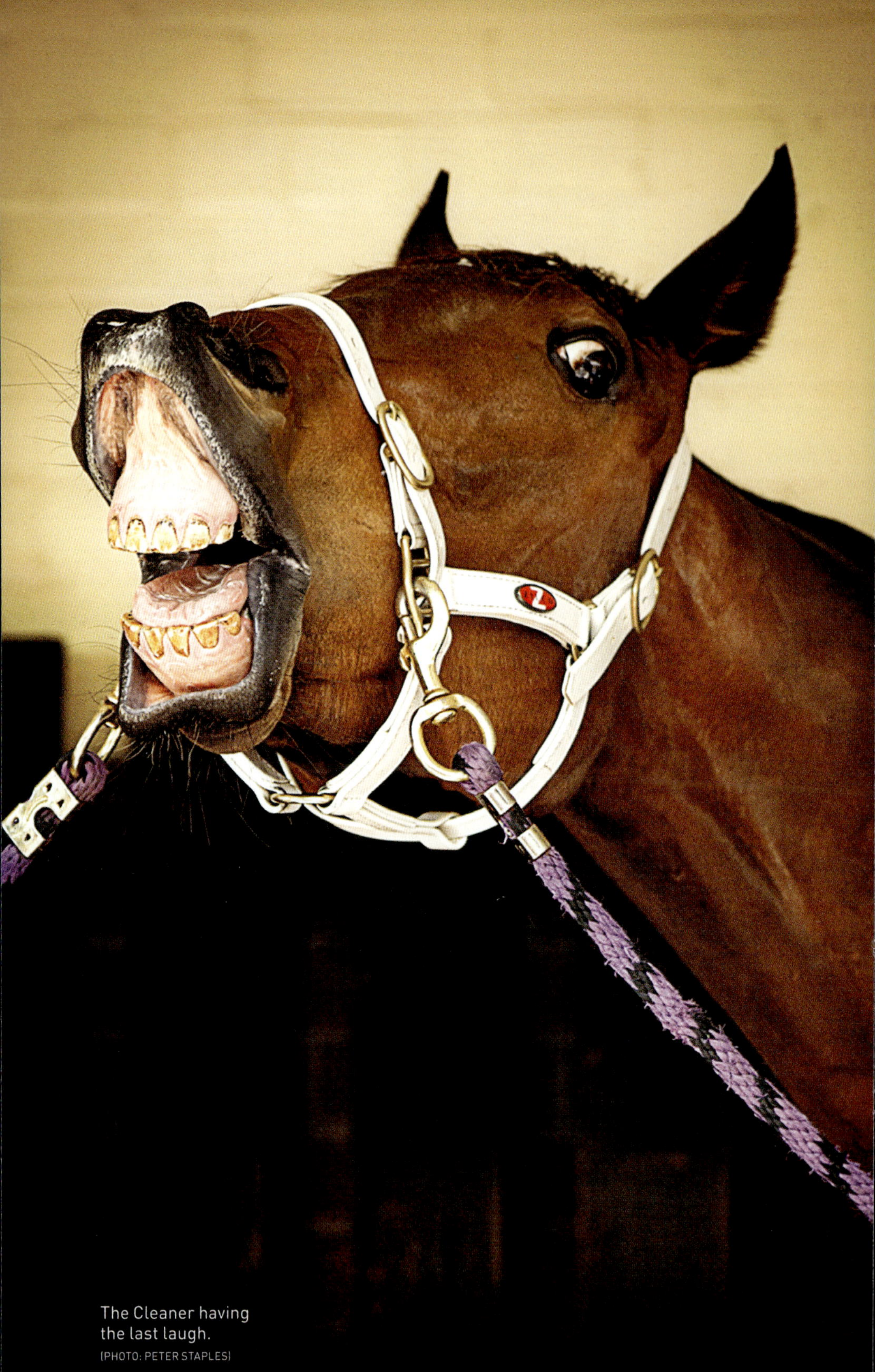

The Cleaner having
the last laugh.
(PHOTO: PETER STAPLES)

off to their new abode with the prospects of building on the bank balance that was bulging, courtesy of a handy profit on the Penguin property.

"Lyn was on board with the move because I could earn nearly double what I was earning at the paper mill. I was on between $500 and $600 a week at the mill and that was with heaps of overtime but I could pick up $1000 a week as a share-farmer. I'd be working seven days a week but it was worth having a crack and I was still able to play footy. We were moving into a nice house and that pleased Lyn. She was a good home maker and it didn't take her long to make it very comfortable."

Share farming was common in the 1970s and 80s but the deals struck by the land owners back then were not as lucrative for the share farmer as they are in today's market. Mick received one third of the profits from whatever he helped produce on the farm with the milk products the mainstay of the business. The money rolled in for only nine months a year and the other three was spent cutting hay and attending to other menial tasks that formed part of the contract.

Share-farming remains a key part of the dairy industry, with almost a fifth of Australia's 6400 dairy farm businesses operating under share-farming arrangements at the end of the 2015-16 financial year. In most cases farm owners take on a share-farmer as a first step towards farm succession or to reduce their involvement in the day-to-day operations of the farm. Professional farm managers also see share-farming as the next step in their careers. The financial arrangements can work out well for both the dairy owner and the share-farmer but there is also some risk for both parties.

"It was a job that required a lot of work and the hours were long but the return was pretty good. I'd be up at 4am to let the dogs loose. They would go and round up the cows and head them to the milking shed. While that was going on I'd be firing up the milking machines and running hot water through each one to make sure they were clean and then I'd start hooking the cows up to the machines. After two hours or so I'd put the cows back in the paddocks and get them fed out, clean the machines then head back home for some breakfast.

"After brekky I'd tend to the crops or anything else that needed to be done around the property like mending fences or checking the machinery. There was always something to do on a farm and basically the harder you worked the more you earned. At least that's what is supposed to happen but somehow it never quite worked out that way."

IT was at Wadley farm in 1976 that Lyn fell ill and doctors were unable to diagnose the problem. What started out as a common cold deteriorated rapidly into constant nausea and incredibly bad stomach pain. Weight was falling off her at a rapid rate.

"I knew Lyn was crook because she had cut her smoking right back and she wasn't eating much. One day Mrs Wadley ran to the milking shed and said I'd better get home because Lyn had collapsed. Kim had called the farm so I rushed home and found Lyn lying on the kitchen floor writhing in pain. I took her to the hospital and even the specialists couldn't tell her what the problem was. She had test after test but whatever they were testing her for kept coming back negative. Whatever it was almost killed her but one day she woke up and said she felt a lot better and she never looked back."

Lyn was a strong-willed woman; this was one of the things that attracted Mick to her in the first pace. She was very caring but also was quick to unleash a venomous tongue on anyone who did her wrong. Later in the marriage Mick was to fall victim to her wrath. Mick recalls one episode that involved Lyn and the family car.

"Lyn never bothered to get her driver's licence; she probably preferred to be chauffeured around everywhere and that way she could have a drink without ever having to worry about being sober enough to drive home—she left that to me.

"One day she asked if I'd take her down to the local pub and I refused so she grabbed the car keys and jumped in the car and said she would drive herself and that I could come and pick her up if she was too pissed to drive home. She got as far as the first turn in the road and almost flipped the car on its roof when she drove it into a ditch. The car was stuck in the ditch and she had no idea what to do to sort it out. Instead of helping her out of the car I just stood there pissing myself laughing and then she let me have it. Lyn could swear when she wanted to but that day I heard words come out of her mouth that I never heard her say ever again."

Mick let her sit there for a while before he jumped in the car, pushed Lyn into the passenger seat, slipped it into to reverse gear then drove to the pub. Mick stayed and they had an afternoon session on the grog and had a good laugh about her first attempt at driving a car.

6

On the Move

NOT long after Lyn had recovered from her mystery illness Wadley decided to abandon the dairy farm and concentrate on producing a fat cow business but Mick was already aware of the plan and he had been making inquiries about future employment. Before the last milk payment had hit the bank he was signing on the dotted line to take up a share-farming role at Don Lowe's Bowthorpe Dairy Farm at Longford, right in the heart of Tasmania's thoroughbred breeding country. The contract was to manage a similar-sized farm with the same number of cows but fewer crops, an arrangement that suited Mick. As a bonus the contract included a three-bedroom home on the property.

By this time Mick had refined his punting skills with some decent collects ensuring new school uniforms for the kids instead of hand-me-downs, so life in the Burles camp was rosy.

Although most of Mick's punting investments were on interstate racing he had started to take an interest in the local product. Punting came first, but he had an urge to own a racehorse. After he confessed to Lyn he was thinking about buying a galloper she all but threatened to leave him if he ever spent any of their money on a racehorse. To Lyn such an investment was pure folly. But Mick had a plan to achieve his desired result and it worked like a charm.

"I reckoned that I could get away with buying a racehorse if I put it in Lyn's name. So I went looking for a suitable horse to buy and one of our greatest jockeys of all time, Max Baker, heard I was on the lookout for a nag and he suggested I buy a three-year-old filly called Robin's Gamble, for sale for $1000. He reckoned it was no star but would definitely win a race or two."

The day after Mick handed over the grand for Robin's Gamble, Don Lowe collared Mick and asked if it was true that he was interested in buying a racehorse. The conversation that followed may haunt Mick until the day he dies.

Lowe was also a thoroughbred breeder and he had enjoyed his share of success with Bowthorpe-bred stock. One of his fillies to be sold at the yearling sale used to wander into the paddocks that housed the cows.

"Every time I'd bend down when this grey filly was in the paddock, she'd come up and bite me on the arse," Mick said. "She was a real uppity filly and even though she was probably only being playful I hated her because she'd never miss me. So when Don asked me if I was interested in buying a racehorse I said I had already bought one the day before. He asked me how much I'd paid and I told him and then he said I could have bought this grey filly that had failed to bring her reserve at the upcoming yearling sale for $5000 and that I could have paid it off a month at a time out of my wages.

"Bugger me if it he wasn't talking about the filly that kept biting me. So I told him in no uncertain terms what he could do with the grey filly. Unfortunately for me that filly went on to become Bow Mistress, who was one of the best-performed handicap and weight-for-age sprinters Tasmania has ever produced. Every time I look back on that day I give myself a mental boot up the arse."

Bow Mistress did have an outstanding career. She had 40 starts for

12 wins and 11 minor placings with seven of her wins coming in Tasmania from 14 outings when in the care of Tasmanian Racing Hall of Fame trainer Claude Best. Her biggest win in Tasmania was the Thousand Guineas at three, one of five wins that season over distances ranging from 1000 metres to 1600 metres.

Lowe sent her to Melbourne in the Autumn of 1983 to be prepared by the late Alan 'Meggs' Elkington and she announced her arrival on the national stage with a first-up win in a Listed race for three-year-olds over 1200 metres at Flemington in June 1983. Her first mainland campaign ended two starts later with a close second at the same track. She won first-up as a four-year-old at Caulfield and went on to finish fourth to River Rough in a Pure Pak Stakes and second to Keepers in the Linlithgow Stakes before a close-up third in a Group 1 Oakleigh Plate won by Mighty Avalanche.

Bow Mistress produced her biggest win as a five-year-old by winning the 1984 weight-for-age J. J. Liston Stakes (then G2) at Caulfield and she followed up with a luckless third in the (then) G2 Memsie Stakes. Her form waned but when she appeared for another campaign as a seven-year-old she won the St Aubin Handicap first-up at Sandown before finishing last of 17 at her second attempt at winning a Liston Stakes. In her swan song she was a close second to Delightful Belle in the Memsie Stakes to end her career with stake earnings of almost $126,000, three Listed wins, and one at Group 2 level.

To add more to Mick's grief, each year in February, the Bow Mistress Trophy is run during the Hobart Carnival. It is one of only four Group 3 races held in Tasmania.

WITH the sale docket for Robin's Gamble tucked into one of the secret compartments of his wallet Mick delivered the news to Lyn that he had bought her a racehorse. The abuse he was expecting never came. "When I told Lyn I'd bought the horse for her there was this awkward silence and that's when I broke out into a sweat because she didn't carry on much at all. In fact she was quite calm and I just thought to myself what a clever bastard I was. I made arrangements for the whole family to go and see the horse that weekend. The mare was stabled with Cliff Perry and I'd wised him up on the ownership arrangements just in case he let something slip that might cause me a bit of grief."

Mick, by this stage, had a burning ambition to become a trainer. He had been around horses all his life and he was a sponge whenever he spent time with local trainers. Many trainers, including Graeme McCulloch, who operated a successful training and horse breeding operation at Whitemore, took a shine to Mick and some solid friendships were formed.

The trip to the stables at Longford had Lyn in raptures over her new interest but while she stood ogling the powerfully-built filly Mick was eyeing off another filly Perry had for sale. A week later he became the owner of Lady Vale for what he reckoned was a bargain at $600.

"I didn't have too much a problem telling Lyn I'd bought another horse, after all she had one so I told her it was only fair that I should have my own so everything was sweet and away we went. The horses were being trained by Cliff Perry but one day I went to the stables and found them almost knee deep in mud so I made arrangements to have them sent to another trainer. I sent them to Graeme McCulloch who had become a good friend and he prepared them both."

Robin's Gamble had a couple of starts for one minor placing but when she lined up in a maiden in Hobart the trainer thought she could win, the race coincided with Lyn's sister Jodi's wedding in Burnie so neither of them could attend the meeting.

Champion Tasmanian jockey Geoff Prouse was booked for the ride and he had rung Mick during the week to tell him that he thought the filly was a 'good thing' because the field was weak and if he rode her a certain way they wouldn't beat her. Mick hung off every word and took the rider's appraisal as gospel and passed it on to Lyn who told anybody who would listen that her horse would win.

The wedding ceremony was scheduled to start at 2pm and Robin's

Gamble's race was at 1.30 so everyone at the church was gathered around a car radio that became the central speaker system for the race broadcast. As the field wheeled around the home turn Prouse had made his move from back in the field to have the filly poised behind the leaders at the top of the straight and when he called on the filly for the supreme effort she responded magnificently and powered her way to an impressive win.

"When the filly won Lyn was running around like a mad hatter kissing and hugging anyone who'd let her. I just stood back and took it all in. I don't think she ever smiled that much again. Even the kids were doing a jig out the front of the church. It was a pretty good night, from what I can remember of it."

When the winner's cheque was posted out Mick had some reservations about handing it over. Telling Lyn the horse was in her name and that he had bought it for her was one thing but handing over the prizemoney after he'd been paying all the bills was another matter; but to keep the peace he cashed the cheque, put the money in an envelope and handed it over.

"The look on Lyn's face when she opened the envelope was worth its weight in gold but there were no more wins for the filly and as for my bargain buy, well that was a disaster. It turned out Lady Vale couldn't get out of her own way. She was absolutely hopeless and never raced and I ended up giving her away as a pony club hack."

The horse ownership bug had bitten Mick but not to the point where he was prepared to make any more investments in the short term given the disappointment with Lady Vale and the subsequent failures of Robin's Gamble.

7

Down Times

IT was 1980 and the dawn of a new era for the Burles family. The share-farm business at Bowthorpe was all Mick had expected and the children were happy living a semi-rural life with eldest son Kim, now aged eight, rising early most mornings to gather the cows for milking with his trusty dog Shadow by his side. Kim and his Dad working together helped bond the family unit. Sometimes Damien would tag along, although Kim regarded his presence as a bit of an intrusion on his special time with his Dad.

Mick and Lyn were strong characters and while they loved each other and showed all the affection they thought was needed towards their three children, a sinister element was lurking in the background; it involved alcohol and gambling. Lyn was becoming more reliant on a drink to get her through the day while Mick's gambling had stepped up a few notches to the point where he was visiting the local TAB more than once a week.

"I knew Lyn's drinking was getting worse but I couldn't complain too much because I was starting to gamble more but I honestly felt that I had it under control. Lyn would complain about my gambling and I'd just tell her what I thought about her drinking and that would usually end up in an almighty blue but we'd go to bed and get up the next morning as if it never happened and that went on for ages."

The sudden death of Lyn's youngest sister Peta at age 33 hit the family hard and in particular Lyn who was as close to her as any sister could be. Peta had been feeling ill and the day she visited the local GP she was complaining of chest pains. After taking a few steps outside the surgery she dropped dead after suffering a heart attack.

"Lyn was devastated and it definitely sent her further into the bottle," recalled Mick.

Mick remained happy with his lot at Bowthorpe and life progressed without much change until the day Mick refused an instruction from Lowe to cut hay for some of his family and friends.

"As part of my contract I had to cut hay for the farm so I'd managed to cut 900 small bales and X number of large and that was all we needed for farm use but Don said he had promised some friends and family members some hay and that I had to cut it. I told him we already had all we needed for the farm and if he wanted any for his friends he could cut it himself.

"He got real shitty about that and after a few more attempts to get me to do it he came down and said I'd better leave to which I told him I was going nowhere until I got all the money I was owed. I told Lyn we'd sit it out for a couple of days because he still owed me a fair bit of money.

"In the end it all came down to an interpretation of the contract. He said I'd broken the agreement and for that I'd have to pay. I sought legal advice and we started proceedings that would hopefully ensure I was paid what I was owed."

Mick was in a spot of bother financially but somehow he managed to secure a bank loan to buy a house in Longford for $25,000 even though he'd just lost his job. The family was forced to live in a caravan for about a month while the paperwork was processed for the purchase of a neat weatherboard home in Godrick Street, not far from the Longford Racecourse.

In order to survive Mick applied for the dole. With three children to support he had enough to pay a mortgage and feed the family with very little left over for life's luxuries. For eight months he and Lyn survived on the hope that the money Mick claimed he was owed would enable them to get back to a reasonably comfortable existence.

"I guess I was living in hope that the right thing would be done but in the end I was told that if I wanted to pursue the money owed it would end up costing me more in legal fees, so I had to let it go."

By this time Mick had become tired of the dole and decided it was time to find work, so after a few phone calls he secured a job as a truck driver carting freight between Launceston and Hobart, with the odd interstate trip thrown in for good measure. But no sooner had he passed his test to secure his endorsed truck driver's licence the bank foreclosed on his mortgage and they lost their home. The family was uprooted again and Lyn began to hit the bottle harder than ever.

Mick managed to secure a rental property in Launceston and while it was nothing lavish it was clean and big enough to accommodate the family.

LYN had begun to drink excessively with her favourite Boag's Draught substituted for cheap cask wine, due mainly to a lack of funds. The arguments with Mick were becoming more frequent, so much so that the children were starting to feel the effects of their constant bickering and shouting matches. Mick was back on the punt trying to win big to keep the family afloat but like all gambling addicts he was clutching at straws to justify his habit. Family and friends could see the family unit starting to crumble.

"Some nights I'd come home from a long day at work and Lyn would be passed out in the bath and the kids would be waiting for me to cook a meal. I didn't mind doing that because I was a dab hand in the kitchen. And the kids were happy because while Lyn was asleep there was no arguing."

While Mick pursued some part-time work to help supplement the income Lyn remained committed to tending to the household chores. When she was sober, life in the Burles household was pleasant enough but as soon as Mick arrived home and she'd had a belly full of beer or wine they would be exchanging barbs that would lead to full-voice arguments and it would always be about Mick's gambling and how it had destroyed their lives.

Mick would reciprocate by blaming most of the problems they had on Lyn's addiction to alcohol. Somehow during this convoluted relationship Lyn fell pregnant and the arrival of Dion in 1985 helped ease the storm. Lyn eased up on the drink and Mick tried to curb his gambling that had by this time started to consume him.

"There's no doubt the arrival of Dion was a surprise but I can remember everything being rosy in the last few months of the pregnancy because she was off the grog and I'd even eased up on the punt and for a moment there I thought we probably still had a chance of keeping our marriage together and it got even better after Dion was born."

The house at Elphin Road in Launceston was comfortable, but Mick wasn't sure what the future might hold because there was talk of the house being sold, so he made application for a Housing Commission home and he was put on a waiting list.

"I had to do something about getting a permanent home for us and with the bank having repossessed our place at Longford I had no hope of getting another loan, so I thought the next best thing was to get a Commission home. I knew there were a few coming up at Ravenswood on the other side of town (Launceston). It took a while but we eventually got onto a short list and soon after, we moved into a house at Ravenswood. The rent was cheap and it was close to schools. That was a big load off my mind."

Once the new house was sorted Mick picked up a couple of part-time jobs that had the potential to put the family on easy street but all it did was give him more money to play with at the TAB. He started punting horses every day and while he picked up a good amount of what he called big wins of over $1000 in a day, by the end of the week he'd be struggling to find a spare $5 that one of his sons needed for a school excursion.

"The gambling thing was a problem and when I look back on what I was doing with my money I can understand why Lyn was so pissed off but I kept using the excuse that because I didn't drink I could spend as much or more on the punt because at least I had a chance of getting my money back.

"By this time I was working for Hammonds as a semi driver carting freight during the day Monday to Friday and then I'd go and work in a bar for three hours three nights a week and four nights a week I had a job cleaning at a school. I don't remember how much I was bringing home each week but it was enough to make sure the family was well fed but if I had only tucked some away instead of blowing it as soon as it hit my pocket I'd be a bloody millionaire today.

"If I had a big win on the punt I'd spend it so they couldn't get it back. There was one time I ran new carpet through the house after a big win and bought a new lounge suite and television. The whole family knew when I'd struck a big win on the punt."

But Mick's job with the Transport company gave him too many opportunities to feed his punting habit. It would be nothing for Mick to pick up his pay packet at the depot and by the time he'd done three trips either between Launceston and Hobart or Launceston and Burnie he'd have disposed of the lot with the beneficiaries being his favourite TABs along either route.

"I'd punt my wages from my day job but I knew I had another two part-time jobs to fall back on and the money I earned from those jobs would pay the rent and keep the wolves from the door and to make sure Lyn had enough grog in the house to keep her going.

"It was only the times when I was real short of cash that Lyn and I had our biggest arguments. She'd scream at me about all the money I was wasting on punting the horses then I'd have a crack at her about the drinking then in the end I'd tell her to have another drink and shut up."

MICK'S life at home was worsening by the day, one of the reasons he chose to work so many jobs. He also was nearing the end of his playing career with the Northern Districts Football Club so he turned his focus to coaching and also decided to offer his services on the committee.

"The club didn't have much money, in fact it was nearly broke. There was never enough money to pay for some decent players who would give the club a chance of winning games and as for playing finals football that was completely out of the question. The club needed money to be competitive so I was at a committee meeting one night and when the chairman asked what we could do to raise some decent money I suggested we go back to an old method and that was to run strip nights or even jelly wrestling. I'd been to one and the place was packed to the rafters. I thought it was like a licence to print money.

"The chairman asked how they could go about organising a jelly wrestling event and I said just leave it to me, I'll do it. So I put an ad in the paper calling for women who'd be interested in jumping into a ring covered in jelly dressed in a bikini. I had about 50 calls and I only needed 12 girls. I was able to pick a good group and a nice cross section of shapes and sizes."

To put on the show, he needed a centrally-located venue that could accommodate up to 400 people. He didn't have to look far because one of the club's sponsors was the Townhouse Hotel in Brisbane Street, Launceston.

"I had to find the proper industrial jelly to use and that wasn't cheap because we needed so much to cover an area that was the size of a normal boxing ring only at ground level with sides about two foot high and the jelly had to be about eight inches deep. Once I had all that organised we set a date. The boss of the hotel advertised the show and we had a full house on the first night and I think they charged $10 a head so the pub covered the costs and made heaps over the bar. Everything went like clockwork and we raised a bucket load of money. The girls were all keen to keep doing it because we had it well organised and I paid them good money."

Mick had struck gold with his fundraising idea and word soon spread around the clubs that Mick's jelly wrestling was well worth a look. But it wasn't enough for Mick so he introduced strippers into the act and before he knew it he had a thriving business. He charged between $3000 and $4000 per show which left a tidy profit for the football club after all expenses were covered and that included at least $100 each for the entertainers.

"It was a great show because all the girls would be dressed in bikinis and they'd jump into the ring and the first one to lose her bikini top or bottom was the loser and we'd have six bouts and then elimination finals to find an overall winner. The strip shows were good too but not as much fun as the jelly wrestling. The word spread like wildfire.

"All these footy clubs and other sports clubs were wanting to buy the show and I remember taking it to the Menai Hotel in Burnie and about 1600 people lined up in the street to get tickets so the pub manager asked if we'd do two shows and when he said he'd pay us the same amount for the extra show the girls agreed and that was a mega night for everyone because the pub was charging $15 a head and they somehow fitted 500 people in for each show.

"We worked well as a team and I always made sure the girls were looked after at all the venues with strict security a must because some of the blokes at those places could get a bit carried away when they got pissed but none of the girls ever felt threatened.

"I remember one night I was fixing something in their change room while they were on stage and when they came back in they just started taking their clothes off as if I wasn't there. We just had a mutual respect for each other. I suppose if I was ever going to be unfaithful to Lyn it was while I was running those shows around the state but that's one thing I can say with all honesty I never played up on my wife, even when the well had dried up at home.

"I'd tried to make sure all the girls looked the part and the dozen I picked in the beginning were all very fit and by the time we'd done a few shows they were real professionals. I ended up with about 18 on the books and a few of them did both stripping and jelly wrestling.

"It was amazing really to think that I could put it all together and it had the potential to make the footy club a lot of money. But after a few shows I asked how the club was placed to pay some decent money for a few players and I was told somebody had broken into the secretary's office and stolen the cash. I told them to stick it up their arse after that and I never organised another show. The girls were disappointed and surprisingly nobody else wanted to take it on."

8

Leaving Home

IT was February 1990 when Mick made a decision that would change his and his family's life. Before he left for work two days before Carissa returned to Queechy High School to start grade nine, Mick summoned the three children still living at Ravenswood for a chat about a plan he had to try and make their lives more comfortable.

By this time eldest son Kim had flown the coop. He had left school as soon as he turned 15 to take up a job as an apprentice boiler maker/ welder with the Tasmanian Railways. But a year later he had enough money to support himself, so he left home. Mick told the children that he was planning to leave the family unit. His exit plan was simple and all he hoped was that the children would understand his reasoning, after all walking out on his kids would not be seen in the best light by his family and friends. It was a hard pill to swallow for Mick but he felt it was the only way he could save his children from any more suffering.

"It had reached a stage that Lyn and I would be arguing non stop. I'd come home from work and often with a load of groceries and meat for the freezer, but as soon as I stepped foot in the door she'd be on the attack. She would usually have downed at least three or four long necks of beer or a cask of wine by the time I got home and she'd start on me. She was almost delusional, accusing me of sleeping with all these other sheilas and then she'd turn on my punting. I felt the only way the kids were ever going to get any sort of peace was if I left."

Mick explained to Damien, who was then 16 and Carissa, 14, that he needed to leave the family unit for their sake as well as their mother's. And while they didn't fully comprehend the necessity of his actions they got the general idea. Even Dion, the youngest, had an inkling that it might be for the best.

"I promised the kids that I'd never be too far away and that they could always rely on me if they needed anything but they were not to tell their mother where I had gone. The kids even helped me pack a suitcase and placed it outside the back door. I told Lyn I was going down to the shop to buy a packet of smokes and I never went back."

RAISING four children is no easy task for any parent but in the case of Mick and Lyn Burles the ingredients for a happy household had been lost through a toxic mix of gambling and alcohol with the children constantly privy to the dark side of their parents' relationship. Being the only girl, and the apple of her father's eye, Carissa was saddened by her father's decision to leave but deep down she knew it was the only sensible thing to do.

"Mum was an alcoholic and Dad was a gambler and they probably argued about money more than anything else and a lot about us kids, in particular my brother Kim because he was the eldest and Mum would let him get away with a lot more than the rest of us," Carissa said.

"We didn't have the things nearly all the other kids in our neighbourhood had because Mum and Dad couldn't afford to buy us any fancy clothes or fancy shoes and we never got to go to any of the big sports events. We'd go to school and have to listen to the other kids talking about the big games they saw or the big shows they went to over the weekend. Mum and Dad always made sure we were clean and tidy but a lot of my clothes were second hand and in the boys' case hand-me downs. I'd say we led a lower than basic life because things were tough for a long while.

"I remember when Kim went to Sydney for a football tournament in 1983 as part of a team that had something to do with the Tasmanian Aboriginal department and that obviously cost Mum and Dad money so we had to live on scones for a week. Mum was a beautiful lady when she wasn't full of grog but she wasn't the best cook and we could have bounced those scones off the wall. The arguments Mum and Dad had that week flowed thick and fast and there were some rippers."

Despite the arguments and friction that both parents caused because of their addictions Carissa says she loved her parents.

"Let's just say we are not a very emotional family but at the end of the day we love each other and that has developed because of the love our parents had for us. I loved my Mum because she was always there for us kids and it was only when she'd had too much to drink that the trouble started."

Carissa says she rarely cried as a youngster because it wasn't the done thing in the Burles household. Both her parents were old school when it came to manners and etiquette. Having relationship-shattering addictions was hard to take for the children but there was no denying they were taught right from wrong from day one and were made to stick to house rules.

"We were raised not to be emotional because emotion is a sign of weakness and something that people would judge you by and that was drummed into us by Mum and Dad but probably more so by Mum. That was the way they were brought up and they just passed it on to us kids. Truth be known I'm grateful for most of the things my parents taught us and even though they were very strict a lot of it serves us well today.

"I can walk into any restaurant and have as good or better table manners than anyone else there. Mum was so hard on us about table manners but at least we all sat at the dinner table together to have our meals and that was great until the arguments started.

"Mum and Dad had sayings such as 'God gave you a spine bloody use it' and 'God gave you hands to use your knife and fork properly' but one of my favourites from Dad was 'tables were made for glasses not arses' because one of Dad's pet hates was people sitting on a kitchen or dining table. He'd say 'You don't want people squatting their arses where you're going to eat food. It's just not the done thing'."

Although her parents were hard on Carissa there is no doubt she received some favouritism from Mick.

"I was Daddy's girl and always have been and that is probably why my Mum was so strict with me and made me feel as if she favoured the boys. But I think that was Mum's way of making sure I grew up knowing right from wrong and whatever else my parents might have been they were strict and cared a lot for us kids."

When the arguments started, Carissa and Damien made themselves scarce but Carissa recalls one occasion when the threats were so real that she feared the worst.

"There was one occasion that me and my brother would run around the house collecting all the knives and took them out to the yard and buried them because we heard Mum tell Dad she was going to stab him. 'I'll cut your throat you fucking mongrel bastard'—is what she screamed at him so we thought the best thing to do was hide all the knives." Carissa said.

"The abuse was insane because after Mum would tell Dad he was ruining her life and that he was nothing but a bastard for gambling away his wages, Dad would start screaming at her saying stuff like she was a waste of space for spending all of the housekeeping money on booze. That was all after Mum had drunk two bottles of beer but by the time she had knocked off four bottles she'd be accusing Dad of sleeping around and just screaming words for the sake of screaming and eventually she'd go to sleep in the lounge chair."

While the constant war of words led to vehement outpourings of abuse neither Mick or Lyn were physically abusive to each other or towards the children. Although Carissa said one day her Dad pushed her Mum backwards into an empty rubbish bin. "When Mum fell into the rubbish bin she kept calling to us kids to help her get out but dad told us we'd be in trouble if we tried to help her. She eventually worked it out on her own."

Carissa remembers vividly what happened the night her Dad left home (for the first time). "Dad spoke to us kids to let us know what he planned to do and that was to stop living with us to help ease the friction and that we might be better off without him living there. We sort of understood and me and Damien even helped him pack his bags.

"The arguments stopped but for a while Mum drank worse than ever. When Mum was sober and Dad wasn't gambling they got on like a house on fire—they were like two peas in a pod but it's because of what I lived through that I don't gamble because I know what it can do to a person and it's pretty much the same with booze.

"I don't gamble because I like it and I know if I did it regularly it would become an addiction so I force myself not to do it and I only drink alcohol in moderation. I was exposed to what drink and gambling can do to a family at a very young age I only have to think of what it did to Mum and Dad to not get caught up with either.

"Dad left two days before I started grade nine and I can remember coming home from my first day of school and having to cook dinner and do the housework because Mum was drunk. Some days I'd come home and find her asleep in the bath, or flaked out in the hallway. It was a very interesting two years."

Carissa had just turned 17 when she left home after falling pregnant with her first child James, but she remained close to her Mother and her little brother.

"I was pregnant when I left home but I was still going back to the house regularly to do things for Mum and Dion. I wasn't worried about Dion because I knew Mum would wake up to herself if I wasn't there to pick up the pieces every day and I was right because Mum definitely cleaned up her act."

Mick's gambling addiction left scars on those around him, but when he was thrust into the national spotlight through the feats of The Cleaner, all of his children were quick to boast that he was their Dad.

"Being Mick Burles' child gave us kids bragging rights when The Cleaner hit the big time and all of us are very proud of what he's made of his life as a horse trainer. Dad's done a lot of things in his life to earn money to raise a family and while he's had his share of self-inflicted problems he has always been a hard worker and carer to us kids.

"The horses have always come first with Dad. He missed Dion's wedding because The Cleaner was running in a race and he missed his grandson James' wedding because of a horse race, but that's Dad."

MICK has never shied away from a stoush. His upbringing helped build a strong character that prevented him from falling victim to bullies and he still has no sympathy for those who can't or won't stick up for themselves. But when he decided to pack up his belongings and leave a relationship that he had hoped would last a lifetime, he was confused, probably for the first time in his life.

The arguing and discontent had finally taken its toll. He wasn't just leaving the love of his life he was also walking out on his children whose characters he had helped mould. He didn't care what others might think of his actions but the fact that he was walking away from his kids weighed heavily on his conscience. But in the end he was convinced his departure from the family unit was in the best interests of everyone—him included.

"I've done some stupid things in my life but leaving Lyn and the kids wasn't one of them. It was the right thing to do. I remember my mother telling me that crying is a sign of weakness and I probably instilled that in my kids but when I walked out of the house with no intentions of ever going back I cried bucket loads that night.

"My sister knew what had been going on and she was happy for me to stay with her (in Launceston) until I found a place of my own but I knew that if I was just around the corner the temptation to go back would be too great so I decided to take a trip interstate and lay low for a bit."

Mick spent only three weeks in Melbourne but it was long enough for Lyn to realise that the man in her life was serious about the split so she decided she had better clean up her act. Carissa had mixed emotions when her dad walked out.

"When Mum realised that Dad had gone, probably forever, she stopped drinking but I think she did it because she thought it was a way of getting Dad to come back and it almost worked. When Dad found out that she had stopped the booze he came around more often. He wouldn't stay but at least they were back on talking terms and for a while there things were really good and even us kids thought they'd have another go at making it work."

In the first instance Mick and Lyn were attracted to each other because they were opposites. They were strong individuals with neither prepared to relent on major issues that involved the family unit. But when those attitudes are mixed with two of life's great evils there is little hope of a good outcome.

"When I heard from the kids that their Mum had given up drinking and given I'd also woken up to myself and cut my gambling right back I thought I'd give it another shot and Lyn was all for it. When I moved back in I only took a few clothes in a suitcase and I kept up the rent on the flat I'd leased just in case. It was bloody great because we were civil to each other, probably for the first time in years and the kids actually enjoyed us being together again.

"But two weeks in, Lyn turned to me and said that now that I had woken up to myself she would be able to relax and have a drink. That night she got as pissed as a nit. Any chance we had of making it work again flew out the window that night. I said good night to the kids, grabbed my suitcase, put two hundred bucks on the kitchen table and walked out knowing it was all over."

Mick was shattered because he really believed there had been a chance to save their relationship but he had to face up to the fact that, while he was around, Lyn would never stay sober and the kids realised it too.

Mick made sure Lyn and the children knew where he was so he could be contacted any time he was needed, although Mick drew the line when Lyn found a new partner.

"It was a while after we split up that Lyn cottoned on to a bloke who moved in. She rang me one day to say she needed the lawn mower fixed so I told her to get the new bloke in her life to do it. But she said he was a lazy bastard who wasn't into that sort of shit so I told her he mustn't be much chop and that she should piss him off and the next thing I knew he was gone."

9

A New Beginning

AFTER three years of trundling up and down the Midlands Highway delivering freight Mick wanted a change. Through an acquaintance who worked for the Launceston City Council he was told of a street sweeper position that was about to be advertised and as he had all the qualifications he snared the job. He was no stranger to early morning starts having spent about eight years rising before dawn on the farm.

Mick liked the sound of the job because it required 4am starts but that also meant early finishes and that suited him because by this time he had begun showing a lot more interest in becoming a horse trainer. That meant he could visit some of the training establishments in the region and familiarise himself with the day-to-day operation of training racehorses.

While it was still only simmering on the back burner, training racehorses was something Mick had longed for ever since he had bought his first thoroughbred. His affinity with the thoroughbred had been bottled up inside but now there was no reason he had to hide his passion. His commitment to his children never waned and he also ensured Lyn was well supported, albeit depending on what his finances would allow. He took to working three jobs to cover all the bases but that was nothing new to Mick. He had also eased right back on his gambling. All of a sudden he was able to make decisions that weren't based on a need to fuel his addiction so more often than not he had access to cash.

"There was a time when I really had my shit together and even though I had no possessions to speak of other than a second-hand car, I was happy and I had something to focus on. I knew it wouldn't be easy to get a trainer's licence but I was real sure I had what it takes to be a good one."

Mick started to struggle with early morning starts on the street sweeper. With winter approaching he wasn't sure if he could handle another two or three months facing up to temperatures that plummeted to well into the frosty range, so he started looking elsewhere.

"A major industrial contractor Chris Hazelwood put an ad in the paper looking for a street sweeper at Comalco's aluminium plant at Bell Bay. It was for a bit more money and the hours were varied so when I got the job I rented a place in George Town. It meant giving up a couple of my part-time jobs but I knew I could get a job as a barman or a job in a kitchen at one of the pubs in the area.

"I ran the sweeper for a while then one of the bosses asked me if I'd consider making a change. He asked if I'd be interested in vacuuming the big aluminium smelter pots. It was a lot more money and that would mean less part-time work so I took him up on the offer."

TAKING on his new role at Comalco would have a great impact on Mick's life. About six months into the job of vacuuming the giant smelter pots he suffered a serious back injury that at one stage had specialists talking about the possibility that he might end up spending the rest of his life in a wheelchair.

"I was going about my business vacuuming this pot when without warning the pressure went haywire. Apparently a big piece of solid aluminium got stuck half-way up the hose pipe and I was flung up hard against the pot alongside the one I was vacuuming and unable to let go of the hose, I was thrown around like a rag doll.

"The pots are electrified and there were sparks flying all over the joint every time I was thrown up against one but that was all I remember. I woke up in hospital and the X-rays and scans showed I had a half a dozen fractured vertebrae in my back and a few other broken bones. I'd suffered pain before but nothing like that and it took forever to heal."

Unable to return to work Mick spent over a year working through a worker's compensation claim and in late 1995 he was awarded a $150,000 payout. As he had been off work beyond the allowed time under the Worker's Compensation Act he was transferred to a disability pension with those payments deducted from the final settlement.

His rehabilitation was slow and tedious but it also had given him plenty of time to ponder his future. The thought of training racehorses had never left him so armed with a robust bank balance for the first time in his life he chartered a course that would lead him to his ultimate goal.

The first thing he did when the money landed in his bank account was tend to some family needs and that included dishing out cash to all of his children and to Lyn, who he had been seeing on a semi-regular basis since severing the relationship. Neither of them had any intention of filing for divorce.

"I still loved Lyn. We just couldn't live together, so when the money from my payout came through I decided to look after the family by giving them some cash and buy them a few things they needed and then get myself set up."

Mick's car had run its race so he purchased a Ford Fairlane that he was able to secure at the right price from a mate who said he had got it off an old bloke who only ever drove it to church on Sundays. Once he was able to get around without the aid of a walking stick Mick went searching for some more leisure items including a boat and a caravan.

The five-metre Savage runabout with a 100 horsepower Mercury outboard motor accompanied by a *King* tip-tilt trailer was to serve them well and the six-berth caravan found a permanent location at Bakers Beach near Port Sorell, about 15 minutes' drive from Devonport on the north-west coast. It was a popular camping and caravan site and a place that Mick liked to call his second home.

"It was bloody great when I got the boat and caravan because we could all get together and spend some time having fun. Getting together at weekends was great and we had some of our best times together and when the kids had holidays. We always went to Bakers Beach and Lyn absolutely loved the place.

"We spent a lot of time there but one day sticks out more than others. I'd hired what they called a Sea Biscuit which was a blow-up thing with two seats that you towed behind the boat and this day I had Damien and Dion on it and we were travelling about 40kmh when it flipped over.

"We were probably no more than 50 metres off shore but when Dion surfaced he was thrashing his arms around like a mad thing screaming something about sharks and Damien was trying to stop him carrying on and yelling at him to stop causing such a ruckus because he was only attracting the sharks. I just sat back pissing myself laughing and I reckon there were about 50 people on the shore doing the same. I found out later that I'd put too much air in the thing and that made it unstable at high speed. I never have been any good at reading instructions."

Dion refused to get back on the Sea Biscuit but Damien could hardly wait to re-straddle the apparatus to prove he could tame the beast.

BAKERS Beach became the family retreat and even though Mick and Lyn were separated, their times at the poor man's holiday resort helped mend their relationship. However, eldest son Kim would make only cameo appearances at Bakers Beach.

When Kim left home at age 16 it was by mutual agreement between him and the rest of the family. He had taken up an apprenticeship to be a boilermaker/welder with Tasrail so with an income stream he was going to be able to support himself and that was the only reason his mother didn't try to stop him fleeing the family nest.

Kim moved into a house that he shared with two of his mates but it wasn't long before he fell foul of the law. Kim had an addiction to marijuana but he shied away from the more illicit drugs but his addiction to the weed and his love of alcohol proved to be a toxic mix and it eventually led to him spending time in jail.

"Just over a year after I left home I got done for stealing and that was to get money to pay for the drugs and alcohol. I was given a 12-month sentence of which eight months were suspended and I ended up only being inside Hobart's Risdon Prison for three months because I got one month off for good behaviour," Kim said.

When released from jail he went to live with his parents but he couldn't settle and after a few months he headed to Victoria where he worked in orchards picking fruit at Shepparton.

"I went fruit-picking and that gave me just enough money to survive but I had this idea of becoming a cocktail barman so I went to the Gold Coast and I ended up landing a job at the Grape Vine, a nice cocktail bar and that was probably one of the best jobs I ever had.

"But when the bar closed I returned to Tasmania and just did some odd jobs until I got the chance to restart my boiler maker/welder apprenticeship with Temco at Bell Bay."

Kim had been working for Temco for about nine months when he suffered a debilitating injury as a result of a work-related accident.

"I was working on the cranes down at Bell Bay when a big piece of steel fell from three levels above me, and hit me on its way through to the ground. I climbed down the stairs with a busted shoulder and head injuries and was taken to hospital at George Town but they just stitched me up and said I was good to go that day. I should have had surgery to fix the shoulder but it never happened."

A Workers Compensation claim would follow and Kim would receive $250,000 in compensation after which he bought a house in Cressy and a car and made visits to his siblings and parents to hand out some cash, including a sizeable sum he believed he owed his father.

"My childhood was good, probably right up until I first started to use marijuana when I was about 13, and even though I'm still using it on prescription, I can see how it was one of the causes of the mistakes and bad choices I made. But it was the alcohol that really messed me up and that's why I don't touch drink today and haven't done since I was 23."

Kim was a talented footballer in his early teens and that helped him and his dad form a close bond but Kim didn't much enjoy his Dad's punting habits.

"Me and Dad had our disagreements and I know I caused most of them in my teens but one thing Dad did that really annoyed me was the times we'd go for a drive and we'd end up parking outside a TAB and sometimes I'd have to wait a couple of hours for Dad to come out. It really gave me the shits."

10

Starting Out

CHRIS Dockeray, Mick's lawyer who had handled his Workers Compensation case, also had an interest in thoroughbred racing. His family had been involved in the breeding side of the industry for many years so the pair would often spend time chatting about the horses the Dockeray family had bred.

Mick shared with Dockeray his desire to take up training and Dockeray revealed that the family was winding up the business and that he had a few horses he needed to move on. The remaining stock comprised an aged mare in foal and two unbroken youngsters that were reasonably well bred.

"I reckon my eyes lit up like a beacon when Chris told me he had a few horses for sale. He told me who they were by and said he'd let me have the lot for $5000 and I thought that was cheap so I snapped them up. I had to get a fair few things in place before I could take the horses and Chris gave me ample time to get it sorted. It was a bit of a gamble but I wasn't about to let the money burn a hole in my pocket."

The mare, Irish Fleece, had produced three maidens. The two youngsters were fillies with one from Irish Fleece that would be named Wind On Wheels (by Prairie Wind) and another bred from a mare that had been loaned to the Dockeray family for breeding purposes.

Mick spent weeks on the lookout for stables that might also have enough ground to accommodate the mare who wasn't far from dropping her foal. He found the perfect setup for all three horses, only a stone's throw from his house at George Town.

"Tony Krushka was a top trainer-breeder who was winding down his business and his place was just around the corner from where I was living so I was able to rent stables at his place and there was enough room for the mare. I sent the two-year-olds to be broken in and I had everything ready for them when they came back from the breaker.

"In those days you had to work with an experienced trainer for six months before the stewards would issue you with a trainer's licence. I had a great bloke named Ron Riley help me to start with but he retired so I went across to work with Larry Dalco who was a very good trainer. I was with him for more than six months and he was able to teach me all I needed to know to get my licence."

Wind On Wheels, was to be trained by Tony Digney, who was the father of the girlfriend of the lad who was riding Wind on Wheels in trackwork. Mick was playing a hand in the young horse's preparation by riding trackwork but the injuries he sustained in the accident at Comalco prevented him from keeping on as a trackwork rider.

"I loved getting out and riding trackwork but it only lasted a few weeks because with my head bobbing up and down and backwards and forwards the vertebrae I had damaged in my neck and back in the accident just couldn't take the strain. I could do it if I didn't wear a helmet but I wasn't getting on one without a helmet so I had to stop riding."

It was all part of a long learning curve for Mick and all he could think about was one day owning and training his first winner. Wind On Wheels had her first start in Launceston at the end of the 1995-96 season and finished ninth of 14 behind El Univeso in a 2YO maiden but three months later, at her fifth start, she gave Mick his first winner as an owner and did it in style scoring by over three lengths in a fillies and mares maiden over 1200m, at Launceston.

At her next start she was third in a three-year-old class six event over 1100 metres in Launceston but it was behind two very smart fillies in Marrow Match who went on to win the 1997 Tasmanian Oaks for Hall of Fame trainer Barry Campbell. Light Of My Life, trained by another Tasmanian Hall of Fame inductee Gary White, was third.

Light Of My Life was owned by Brian and Pam Higgins who raced some of the best horses to grace the Tasmanian Turf during the 1980s and 90s including dual Launceston Cup winner Free Beer (1995/6). Light Of My Life went on to win nine of her 45 starts. One of her wins was over superstar sprinter-miler Royal Rambo, the winner of 13 Stakes races in Tasmania. Royal Rambo's trainer George Blacker regards him one of the best he ever trained.

"Wind On Wheels was a lovely filly but she went sore and she never fully recovered so we probably never saw the best of her. It was the same story with a few others that passed through the stables over the years but let's face it, this game is just another version of Russian Roulette."

Wind On Wheels never won another race and the other filly never made it to the races but the colt foal dropped by Irish Fleece in November 1995 was to realise Mick's dream. The colt, who was gelded before he was broken in, was named Irish Reaction but it was three years before he made a most unimpressive debut in a 3YO Maiden in Launceston, finishing ninth of 13.

WHEN Mick set his sights on becoming a trainer there was no specific timeframe put in place, in fact he wasn't even sure if he would cut it. But once he had hold of the Dockeray horses, and he could see there were enough people in the game who were prepared to help him weave his way into it, he persevered.

"When I went to Larry Dalco's stables at Mowbray I ended up letting the lease go on the house at George Town and took the caravan down to Larry's and I lived there at the stables. I was comfortable enough and I was right where I needed to be to learn all I had to know to get my licence.

"I wasn't in a hurry and Larry offered me a job as a stablehand. I got to understand more about the game in my time with Larry than with anyone else. When Irish Reaction was ready to be put into training he was the official trainer but I did most of the work and I was very happy with that arrangement.

"The horse had about three months' work before his first start and Sandra McFerran rode him. He finished nearer to last and was beaten about a dozen lengths and because he didn't pull up all that clever I gave him a spell.

"He came back three months later and finished midfield in a maiden at Launceston and then he ran last there a few weeks later. He had three more runs without success so I tipped him out for a spell. It was at the end of that first prep I thought I might have a dud. But one thing this game teaches you is that you have to be patient so I put him in the paddock and while he was having a spell I got my trainer's licence."

Mick had tired of living full-time in the caravan so he was making frequent trips to Ravenswood and spending days at a time with Lyn but there was no talk of reconciliation. The arguments were nowhere near as raucous but they were frequent enough to convince Mick a more permanent berth at 2 Currie Place, Ravenswood was not an option.

Mick had finally achieved his goal and while he had no idea of whether or not he would ever make a living as a horse trainer he was sure he now knew enough about horses to at least have a better than average chance of training winners on a regular basis. Mick entered Irish Reaction for a race in Launceston in June 1999 and when he saddled the now four-year-old gelding up for the second race on the card he was a bit jittery, to say the least.

"I don't remember whether I felt any different when I saddled up the horse but I sure as hell felt the pressure when I legged up Dean Larsson who had never ridden the horse before. I know he asked how the horse had been going and if I thought he could win first-up. I just told him the horse should handle the heavy track and that on his breeding he should be a swimmer in the wet and left it at that."

Irish Reaction relished the heavy conditions as Mick had suggested but what he didn't expect was that the horse would make his rivals look ordinary. He strolled to the front at the top of the home straight and went on to win by more than five lengths. Mick had trained a winner with his first starter as a trainer, a feat that put him in rare company.

"The day Irish Reaction gave me a winner with my first starter as a trainer was a terrific feeling. I couldn't get the smile off my dial. I had a few bucks on him at 10-1 so I at least had enough to give the jockey a sling and go out for tea that night. There's no feeling like it in the world. When you've had a horse from day one and deal with all the shit you have to go through just to get it to the races it's brilliant to see it win a race. It doesn't matter whether it's a crappy maiden or a feature race it's all the same. The prize money's better for the good races but the feeling's just the same."

Mick only gave Irish Reaction three more starts that prep before sending him for a spell but the gelding had spent his penny first-up and was unable to deliver. But during the break Mick had grown his team to a half dozen and that was enough to keep him fed and watered without having to dip into any more of his savings.

Irish Reaction returned eight months later to win second-up on a heavy track in Launceston and this time Mick dug deep into his pockets and placed a bet that netted a sizable return courtesy of the luxury odds of 12/1.

"Irish Reaction was a ripper but I remembered being told when I was just starting out in the game that it doesn't pay to keep a horse when it's past its use by date so when I thought I'd gone as far as I could with Irish Reaction I got in touch with Victorian trainer Peter Fell and I sold the horse to him because he showed interest in him when I took the horse to

Melbourne for one start. I sold him for about $5000 but the horse had done a marvellous job for me and I was sorry to see him go."

Mick also had three horses in his care that were owned by his mate Wes Tyne and although there was no great success with that trio they helped pay the bills, although when he first started training at Mowbray Mick had a backstop to ensure he always had some money feeding into the bank. He operated a catering business working the kitchens at a number of pubs in Launceston.

"I was more of a cook than a chef but I operated the kitchen at a number of pubs and I had a pretty good success rate building the venues up. When I started at the Royal Hotel in Launceston they were doing between 12 and 15 lunches a day and by the time I'd finished with it we were doing 150-160 meals a day. It was a similar story when I was at the Rocherlea Tavern and that was the last pub I worked.

"When I had the success with Irish Reaction I thought to myself 'how easy is this training caper', so I packed it in with the kitchen work and just concentrated on training."

Mick had some good bread and butter horses when he first started out and one that he purchased interstate, Viceroy, proved to be a very good money spinner. "I bought Viceroy for $1800 after he had failed at his first six starts in Victoria. When he arrived he had a swollen knee, and he looked like a cripple when he came off the truck. But I managed to patch him up and he won at his first two starts for me and while I wasn't having too many bets back then (2002) I did have $500 on him at $7 with one of the bookies. He was right shitty when he got up and won. He had given me big overs.

"I didn't have as much on him next start but I had the bet with the same bookie and he got the money again at pretty much the same odds so Viceroy proved to be a very good investment but you wouldn't have given two bob for him when he first arrived at the stable."

Tertian's Doll was another that showed consistency and while she was a nasty type around the stables Mick was prepared to put up with her antics once she found form.

"Tertian's Doll was owned by a lovely woman—Anne Wing—and she ended up winning three and ran quite a few placings (six). I remember her first win in Launceston (September, 2000) when Brendon McCoull rode her. He got off and said she had a future. Her first win was over 1400 metres but her next was over 2100, but then I had trouble finding suitable races for her and that's probably why she only won one more.

"Tertian's Doll would try and bite your head off when you walked past her box but I became a wake-up to her and would just quicken my step up whenever I had to walk past her box. She was all right out of her box but she was a bitch when she was in an enclosed space."

Mick found the going easy for the first couple of years as a trainer and while the winners kept coming he had to learn quickly how to handle the disappointments.

"There's only one thing that stops you from getting depressed in this game and that's getting winners and I always seemed to be able to do that. I had my share of dry spells but when I was at Quarrel's my strike rate was pretty good. I never had any champions. Although one horse I had, Lock Me Away, had the potential to be a superstar."

Lock Me Away won only two of his 13 starts, but Mick just liked his athleticism and the way he carried himself. Like so many other would be stars he had issues and eventually they prevented him from making it.

"Lock Me Away was a lovely animal but he was very highly strung and that's what eventually brought about his demise. We set him for a race in Launceston (January 2002) at his third race start and we backed him at 50-1. We didn't have to have much on at those odds and he won easily.

"But he had a habit of injuring himself and one day he and Tertian's Doll were in the yard untethered and they got spooked by something and Lock Me Away ran straight into a straining post and wrecked his shoulder. We managed to get him back to racing and he won another race but had he not had those issues he could have been a really good horse."

11

Back to Work

MICK spent five years playing around with a handful of horses at Mowbray and while the winners never came as often as he would have liked his entrée into professional horse training would give him the grounding needed to eventually land him in the big league, albeit with just one good horse.

Mick was popular among the training ranks and there was none more fond of the likeable larrikin that the late Alan Stubbs, a multiple premiership-winning trainer. Stubbs, along with George Blacker, ruled the roost at Longford for decades. Stubbs won eight state premierships between 1974 and 1991 and prepared some of the best gallopers Tasmania has produced.

He won four Devonport Cups and as many Newmarket Handicaps as well as a Tasmanian Derby. When Mick's money had run out in 2004 he gave training away and started working for Stubbs as a stable foreman. It took Mick a while to readjust. He'd been his own boss for a number of years and winding back the clock was never going to be an easy process. But Mick and Stubbs were cast from a similar mould so Stubbs was careful not to assert his authority too openly where Mick's duties were concerned.

"I'd had a good run with training but I started to really feel the pinch with money running low, so I sucked it up and bit the bullet. I didn't renew my trainer's licence and I went to work for Stubbsy. Alan and I were alike in a lot of ways so he probably knew how I was feeling and he never dished out orders to me like he did with a lot of the others who worked for him. I knew what I had to do and I became his stable foreman and that suited me right down to the ground."

Mick was living at the stables in a two-room portable home that looked more like a shipping container than a dwelling but Mick was happy to take every day in his stride as he made his way back into the workforce.

By this stage he had dispensed with his caravan, boat and the V8 Ford Fairlane. His possessions now comprised a suitcase full of clothes, work boots, a pair of slippers and a good pair of black shoes to be worn only on special occasions.

"I was reasonably happy working at the stables but after a while I started to see the grim side of Stubbsy. He seemed to hate anyone who worked for him. He was a gruff old bastard and he didn't care who he upset. He reckoned if he was paying the bills he could do and say whatever he liked. He wouldn't tolerate slackers and that's probably why he had such a high turnover of staff.

"We were a lot alike in many ways but I could never treat people like he did when he was in one of his moods. I knew what I had to do and got on with it but when he gave one of his stable hands a spray for messing something up, they more often than not didn't show up for work the next day.

"He had a fair turnover of staff. One jockey who was apprenticed to him, Sarah Zschoke, had a book she kept that had the names of all the people who had worked at the stables while she was with Alan. There were more than 100 names in the book over a period of about four years."

Mick had his share of arguments with Stubbs but it was like water off a duck's back for the two wily veterans who both treated an argument as a sport more than a personal rift. But one day a decision Mick took to stamp his authority on a situation that arose from a conflict with a couple of stable employees would force Mick to pack his bags and move on.

"One morning I was getting some horses ready for trackwork and when one came back from being worked with apprentice Jodi Borrett on top she got off and refused to unsaddle the horse saying it wasn't her job. I told her if she didn't do as I'd asked she could piss off and not bother coming back. She said I couldn't do that so I told her again but this time I wasn't as polite.

"Then another rider Dianne Parish chimes in and said if Jodi goes then she'd go too so I told her the same and that was it as far as I was concerned. They went straight to Alan and told him what I'd done and he came running down to the stables and told me I shouldn't have sacked them. He said I had too much of him in me, but I stuck to my guns and told him I'd have more trackwork riders by the next morning and I did.

"Alan said I just had to apologise to Jodi for swearing and she'd come back to work but I told him I had nothing to apologise for, although I must admit I probably told her to fuck off but it wasn't anything she hadn't already heard a hundred times around the stables."

But Mick's actions bothered Stubbs who masterminded a plan to get him to leave of his own accord because he wouldn't fire him.

"I was unsaddling a horse that had just been on the training track and Alan came over and told me I'd done the wrong thing by getting the girl rider to gallop the horse. I told him the horse just cantered because it had only been back in work a week but he was adamant and kept on about it. I went to his house for breakfast and the girls were there giggling and he was still harping on about it so I just told him I'd had enough of his shit and told him to stick his job.

"He just laughed and started eating his breakfast. I got that mad I stormed out and flung the sliding door shut so hard it smashed the glass. He told me to clean it up so I told him to stick it again and walked out.

"I went to Lyn's that night and stayed a couple of days and the next thing Graeme McCulloch's on the phone asking me to go and work for him because he needed someone to help him through the stud season and to help with his training operation."

MCCULLOCH had made his mark as a talented thoroughbred trainer but it was the breeding side of the industry that interested him more. He has invested heavily in stallions over the years with his well-bred West Quest making his mark as one of the greatest stallions to stand in Tasmania.

McCulloch trained Robin's Gamble to win for Lyn Burles so from that day forward he and Mick shared a special mateship, the kind that lasts forever without having to see each other on a regular basis.

Mick took to his new job like a duck to water and McCulloch was only too pleased to have him on board. He was initially taken on to help McCulloch during the busy stud season which would give him at least three months' work but it ended up lasting 18 months. Six months into the arrangement McCulloch broke his ankle and that laid him up for some time so Mick was asked to stay on.

"Graeme was a very hard worker, probably the hardest worker I have known in the racing game so I enjoyed my time working for him. There was always plenty to do and I lived at Grenville the whole time I worked for him. I lived in the guest quarters behind the main house and it was very comfortable. I probably worked six days a week but it was always interesting. I worked with horses mainly but he also grew crops so I helped out when it was needed in that department.

"When Graeme broke his ankle he only had the cast on two days and he got me to cut it off. I think I used a carving knife and he was dead keen to get rid of it because he said it was driving him crazy."

McCulloch has always got along with Mick and he regards him as one of the real characters of the racing game and one of the most down-to-earth blokes he knows.

"When I got Mick to come and help me out it was probably one of the best moves I've made as far as staffing goes," McCulloch said. Mick is a good horseman, he's honest and he's a hard worker and it's rare to find all of those things in the same person. It's true that I got him to cut the plaster cast off my leg because it was giving me the shits because it was as itchy as all hell and besides that it was slowing me down. I never told the doctors and I just went about doing most things that I would have done normally but without running around the paddocks and getting among the horses. I reckon it was a good move because I never had to go back for any rehabilitation and I get around all right on it these days."

McCulloch has enjoyed a lot of success in recent years as a breeder. He bred 2015 Caulfield Cup winner Mongolian Khan from his resident broodmare Centafit. Mongolian Khan was bred on a share basis with Coolmore Stud using their Shuttle Stallion Holy Roman Emperor so when the colt was a weanling McCulloch placed him in a sale and he purchased (reclaimed) the colt for $9000 and bought out Coolmore's share for $4500. But also at that sale was a couple from New Zealand, Mandy and Courtney Howe, who had gone to the sale specifically to buy the colt.

The Howes, who own Ainsley Downs Stud in NZ, were at the sale to buy the colt but they told McCulloch they would not bid if he wanted to buy him back so they didn't place a bid. McCulloch ended up offering the colt to them on a half-share basis if they wanted to take him back to New Zealand and prepare him for the yearling sale with the proposition of going halves in the sale price. He was knocked down for $140,000 at the NZ Yearling sale and the purchaser went on to sell him at the Karaka ready to run sale and that's where the colt's present owners, the Inner Mongolia Rider Horse Industry, bought him for $220,000.

Mongolian Khan was sent to top NZ trainer Murray Baker, who admitted the colt had a few issues that needed sorting out before he would be a racehorse. But Baker eventually ironed out the chinks and after winning on debut at Te Rapa he had five wins from six starts leading up to the Group 1 NZ Derby which he won convincingly at the end of February 2015. Baker travelled the colt to Australia and at his second Sydney start he delivered a brilliant performance to win the Australian Derby that earned him the title of three-year-old of the year in both New Zealand and Australia and the Horse of the Year crown in NZ. But his best was yet to come.

There was speculation that he might not shine at four but he defied his doubters by winning the 2015 Caulfield Cup. Bookies were running for cover as his price to win the Melbourne Cup was slashed to single figures. Unfortunately, he was stricken with a form of colic as he prepared for the big race and spent hours on an operating table at the Werribee Veterinary Hospital in Victoria where he underwent life-saving surgery. Although he raced the following autumn, he was not the same horse and retired a multiple Group One winner of eight races from 1400m to 2400m, winning in excess of $4 million in prizemoney. He became the first horse since Bonecrusher, 29 years earlier, to win both the ATC Australian Derby and New Zealand Derby. He also is the first horse in history to win the ATC Australian Derby, New Zealand Derby and Caulfield Cup. The stallion was secured by Windsor Park Stud and will stand his first season at the Cambridge nursery in NZ in 2016.

"Every breeder wants to breed a Group 1 winner," said McCulloch, "and to have bred a multiple winner at that level has definitely fulfilled my dream."

Mick was given an option to stay longer at McCulloch's but fate would chime in and deliver Mick a pathway to the stars. His old sparring partner Alan Stubbs delivered a mare to McCulloch's one day and when he was able to grab a quiet moment with Mick he delivered some shattering news. Stubbs revealed that he had cancer and that he probably didn't have long to live. He all but begged Mick to return to his stables so that he had someone he could rely on to run the business.

ALAN Stubbs and Mick had mended the bridge that forced Mick to walk away from the Stubbs stable 18 months earlier. When Stubbs revealed his dilemma Mick told McCulloch that day that he would be finishing up at the end of the month and told him where he was going without mentioning the reason why.

"When Alan told me that the bowel cancer was back and that he probably wouldn't see out another summer I just couldn't let him down. I felt sick in the guts when he told me. It was pretty upsetting because the old bastard had hardly had a sick day in his life and he always looked healthy until that cancer got hold of him. I felt sorry for him but I couldn't help but think that this could happen to me."

Mick was also going through a rough patch with his health at the time Stubbs came calling Mick had been told only three months earlier that he had the first stage of emphysema following a lifetime of heavy smoking. Mick had smoked cigarettes on a regular basis since he was about 13 but until he reached 50 he had felt little or no effects from the addiction.

"The first sign that I was in some strife was when I was coming back from settling some horses into a paddock at McCulloch's. I picked up a bale of hay and after I'd walked about 20 yards I had to stop and take a breather. I was short of breath and I had a dizzy feeling. It happened two or three more times so I carted myself off to the doctor and after a couple of tests she told me I had emphysema. She said that if I stopped smoking there and then it probably wouldn't get any worse but I didn't listen. I never told anyone about it because it's not the sort of thing you want being bandied about, especially in the racing game."

Mick sauntered into Stubbs' stable a few weeks after he handed in his notice and it was as if he'd never been away. Jodi Borrett and Dianne Parish were still riding trackwork along with a couple of new faces, although that was to be expected given the stable's staff turnover rate.

When Mick arrived back at the stables there were some very handy horses in the yard including Miewa's Quest, who had only just started to make a name for himself. Stubbs was still barking orders and having disputes with trackwork riders so nothing had changed in that department. But after a while Stubbs needed more time off and that's when Mick came into his own.

12

Sad Times

MICK had been separated from Lyn for more than a decade but he still had strong feelings for her. In 2004 Lyn was also suffering from chronic emphysema. She too had been a heavy smoker and her condition worsened to the point where Mick had no alternative but to have her admitted into a nursing home.

Carissa had been caring for her mother on a daily basis as well as raising her own family but when Lyn's condition required professional assistance, she agreed to her Mum being placed in a high dependency facility. The Cosgrove Park Nursing Home in Launceston became Lyn's new address. Carissa visited every day and Mick would make his way into the facility at least twice a week to spend time with Lyn, while Kim, Damien and Dion would visit whenever they could. Lyn seemed happy enough although she struggled to get around without the aid of a walker.

About 18 months had passed when Mick received a call from Cosgrove Park to inform him that his wife had died. Her death hit Mick hard, harder than he ever imagined. Instead of him consoling his children it was a role reversal.

"Dad was an absolute mess and I had never seen him cry like he did when he arrived at the nursing home," Carissa said. Dad just couldn't stop crying and that showed just how much he loved her. They loved each other to bits, they just couldn't live together."

There was a big turnout at Lyn's funeral service in Launceston and many of those who filled the pews weren't known to Mick. Many of his racing friends paid their respects and there were even a few who had only made Lyn's acquaintance once or twice but had made the effort out of sheer respect for Mick and his family.

"Lyn was very popular and that was obvious by the number of people who showed up to send her off. I never thought I'd be affected by her death like I was. I knew I still loved her," said Mick. "I haven't been with any other woman since we were married. It's just a shame we couldn't get along living together. Other than a short fling Lyn had with a bloke about two years after we separated she hadn't had any other men in her life. We were a strange pair really."

Lyn's cremation was a private affair and her ashes were placed in an urn that stayed with Carissa until she could determine a suitable place to carry out her mother's wishes to have her remains scattered on water in Launceston. It took until 2015 for all the family to agree that the ashes should be scattered in the river that meanders its way through Cataract Gorge, a popular tourist attraction situated about 1.5 kilometres from Launceston's city centre.

After a period of grieving, Mick returned to the stables and buried himself in his work at the Stubbs stable. He still had to deal with similar issues that led to his departure nearly two years beforehand but at least he had something to focus on instead of thinking of the loss of his wife.

MICK had just started to recover from Lyn's death but within 10 weeks of his wife passing his great mate Alan Stubbs, who was in his 80th year, succumbed to the disease that always promised to cash him out. His departure didn't come as a shock to Mick, as had been the case with Lyn's death, but it was a decent blow all the same. Stubbs' funeral was huge. It was standing room only at the back of the Anglican church at Kings Meadows with plenty of spillage onto the main street.

Everyone who lived in Longford either knew or had heard of Alan Stubbs. He came from a racing family with two of his brothers, jumps jockeys Joe and George, both killed in race falls over the hurdles in Melbourne. His older brother Jack rode trackwork until he was 80. Stubbs' record as a trainer earned him a place in the Tasmanian Thoroughbred Racing Hall of Fame in 2008, joining an elite group who have excelled in their respective categories.

"We all thought Stubbsy would just keep going for years because we reckoned he was too mean to die but he got really crook around Christmas time and about six weeks later he was gone," said Mick. "His wife Nancy took it real hard as we all knew she would but she was hell bent on keeping the business going so she took out her trainer's licence and we kept everything ticking over with the stable operating on her licence.

"She had no idea how to put a bridle on a horse in the beginning," said Mick, "and as for saddling one up, well she was bloody hopeless. But it didn't matter because that 's what we were there for and in the end she started to get the hang of it. We had some good horses in the yard and some nice ones coming through so we all just put our heads down and bums up and ploughed on."

John Farrell was a prominent owner-breeder from Hobart who had enjoyed a lot of success with the Stubbs stable and it was one of his breed, a filly named Vivre La Nett, who showed great promise even though she failed to flatter at her only start as a two-year-old. She was from the first crop of Savoire Vivre, a stallion that arrived with great expectations at Tasmania's premier stud, Armidale, three years earlier. Savoire Vivre was leading first season sire in Tasmania and he has continued to dominate despite having passed on in 2012. Probably his most famous son to the end of the 2015-16 season is The Cleaner.

"Vivre La Nett had a few issues I had to work out when she came back as a three-year-old but once I had that sorted she really hit her straps and won five on the trot.

"Corey Kingston was on when she won her first race for me and Nancy but I booked the Frenchman Remi Tremsal to take over and he stayed with the filly all the way through that campaign. She won the Tasmanian Guineas over 1600 metres and then she probably should have won the Thousand Guineas (1600m) that was against her own sex but she was beaten narrowly by a good one from Johnny Blacker's yard (Butzie)."

Mick declared Vivre La Nett would win the Thousand Guineas to whoever would listen and she started the $1.70 favourite but Tremsal had some explaining to do when he returned to the unsaddling enclosure. "On a scale of 1-10 I rated his ride a one." Mick said.

But there were no complaints from the owner given Tremsal's superb handling of the filly at her four previous outings. However, Mick's comments gave credence to the age old saying that a jockey is only as good as his last ride. Tremsal retained the ride for the filly's test over ground in the Strutt Stakes (2100m) in what is the traditional lead-up race to the Tasmanian Oaks. She finished seventh of 15, beaten about four lengths but it was clear she didn't get the trip so she was tipped out for a spell.

MICK was now starting to get the urge to branch out on his own again. The success of Vivre Le Nett gave him a buzz but when the media gathered around the winner's stall after she had won the Tasmanian Guineas he couldn't help but feel slightly left out given he'd put just about all the work into preparing the filly, but was getting none of the plaudits. It was Mick who had sorted out her problems and got her to the stage where she dominated 3YO feature races. But he refused to leave Nancy in the lurch.

"I was happy enough doing what I was doing and sure it was hard at times to sit back and let Nancy deal with the media after the big wins but

I just had to suck it up and ignore it. If I wanted the kudos I could go out and get a licence and train in my own right. It was my choice to be the stable foreman so in the end I just accepted it for what it was."

Mick worked with Nancy until she decided, in August 2008, that she'd had enough of the training caper. She would bow out in style. "I wanted to keep the business going," she said, "so I thought I'd have a go at training but in the end I realised, with my placid nature, I wasn't tough enough to deal with everything that goes with training horses. The people are all different and when things had to be done I wasn't able to get the job done like Alan could.

"I missed Alan terribly and that made it even harder to keep up the training licence. It brought me to tears more than once and I can remember wishing I had him to talk to just to run things by him and get his opinion. He lived racing and I don't think there was a day in his life when he wasn't dealing with or thinking about a horse. He could see things in horses that others couldn't. It's not something anyone can teach you, you either have it or you don't. He could tell if a horse had a problem just by looking at it. He was an amazing trainer."

When Nancy Stubbs decided to give up on training she was approached by another veteran Longford trainer Ken Hanson who was very keen to lease her stables. She agreed and this left Mick, who was keen to renew his license, with the option to lease boxes from Hanson, an arrangement that didn't please him. When Mick was offered stables at Pat Quarrel's at Lonford, he felt he had no option but to relocate.

13

On the Job

TASMANIAN breeder and hobby trainer Pat Quarrel's 15 boxes were on a decent piece of ground just up the road and diagonally opposite George Blacker's training complex at Longford. The yard was big enough for Mick to train and educate horses so he packed his bags and moved in.

"I went to Pat Quarrel's place and while the stables weren't as well cared for as Stubbsy's they were adequate and the rent was cheap. I had a fair few of John Farrell's horses to take with me so there were winners on a regular basis. I was just pleased to be on my own without any of the hassles that came with having two trainers in the one stable complex. I'm sure Ken (Hanson) felt the same with me out of his hair. We'd argue at the drop of a hat and that was no good for either of us."

Mick pottered about in his own world building his team. He went though a lean patch but he had enough horses in work to turn over a tiny profit each month. By this time he had given up on the punt. The days of investing wages at the TAB were well gone but although he was partial to a game of Keno at the local pub he managed to keep that to a minimum.

"When I went back to work for Stubbsy I had pretty much given up betting on horses. I sat down one day and worked out how much I'd spent on punting over the years and when I added up how much I'd spent on the punt and smokes I almost keeled over.

"I'd been working three jobs and almost killing myself with work to feed two habits. I'd gone off my tree when my eldest son got involved with drugs and I even took to him with a belt once to try and straighten him out. But I'd been doing the same or worse and that scared me. I gave away the gambling but I was still hooked on smokes."

Mick's health took a turn for the worse just after he moved into the Quarrel yard. The emphysema was starting to make an impact on his lifestyle but he persisted with the smoking. Sleepless nights were becoming common through his inability to breathe freely with the congestion in his chest building to a point where he required regular trips to his local doctor for a remedy.

"I couldn't give the fags away. I tried my arse off. I'd go two or three days without a smoke but then a horse would play up or someone would upset me and I'd go out and buy a packet of smokes and that would be the end of it. I'd be back smoking a pack a day."

At this stage his emphysema was not interfering with his workload. He paid no attention to early morning starts, after all he'd been rising before the sun poked its nose above the horizon for the best part of his life and while he never liked winter he was still able to deal with the sub zero temperatures that prevail in Longford in June and July.

14

Lot 3, a Feisty Colt

MICK was always on the lookout for young horses that might make the grade. He was a regular at the Tasmanian Magic Millions Yearling Sale and in 2009 he had clawed his way through the catalogue and come up with a handful of youngsters that he thought might make their way into his yard. He had owners waiting in the wings who had told him they were keen to invest and he also had a couple of fledgling owners keen to get on the train. Mick was particularly keen on seeing Lot 3, a colt by Savoire Vivre out of Dash Of Scotch, a Blessington mare who had produced Private Nip, the winner of the Thousand Guineas (1600m) at Hobart in 2000, and the 2002 Hobart Guineas winner (2100m), Strait Dash. Lot 3 was her ninth foal, and her third by Savoir Faire. Lot 3's siblings, Babar and Fine Dimple were nothing special. Babar never made it to the track and Fine Dimple won two lowly races from 21 starts.

Mick was anxious to find at least one yearling that might eventually pay its way and show enough potential to keep his dream alive. He needed to be mindful of his bank balance before engaging in any bidding war but with 16 horses in work and a steady income he thought he was well-armed for any sale ring battle. The flighty colt from Dash of Scotch gave a cheeky squeal when taken out of his box to be paraded before Mick for the first time.

"I'd marked Lot 3 as a definite one to have a look at and there were about four others I thought might be in my price range but this Dash Of Scotch colt was the first I went to see. He was a bit of an upstart and that appealed to me because he showed he had a bit of character and that's one of the first things I look for in a young horse. He was very athletic and was an all round good type but I had him put back in his box and went to look at some other lots I was interested in."

But when he returned for a second look at the colt with attitude, he looked more at what he offered athletically than his character. The colt pranced about like a ballerina, light on his feet but with perfect balance, another characteristic Mick looked for in a young horse.

"I had a close look at him not just the little show off upstart he presented the first time he was paraded. I ran my hands over him and he ticked all the right boxes. He had a nice jaw, a deep girth and I could see his eyes when standing behind him. But when I went back to look at him a third time he trotted up and down with an air of confidence about him that set him apart from all the others I'd looked at. I decided he'd be at the top of the shopping list."

When the colt was presented in the sale ring Mick was hoping to win the bidding but he knew there were others interested. In particular, he knew one prominent buyer had an open cheque book. Mick might be a dreamer at heart but he's also a realist, an important safeguard when horse hunting. For all that, there was something in the breeding of Lot 3 that stirred his emotions. He was ready to take a punt even if the bidding soared beyond expectations.

"There's something about a yearling sale that gets your heart revved up and when you set your mind on buying one it's hard not to get caught up in the excitement. I still get a buzz at yearling sales. It's the thrill of the chase and before you know it you're going in over your head. I've been around long enough to know when to stop these days but there were times when I just couldn't help myself. More than a couple of times I've ended up with one that was overpriced and I'd end up owning half or all of it. Of course it would turn out to be a dud."

As Lot 3, on offer from Armidale Stud, entered the ring and the auctioneer started to reel off the colt's impressive pedigree Mick was leaning up against a steel girder that helped form the framework of the sale ring. The colt, bred by Owen Atkins at Deloraine, had a modest reserve and the bidding started at $2000 a bid delivered by Mick. The bids rose in $2000 lots and as luck would have it Mick's bid of $10,000, the fifth in the short-lived frenzy, saw the colt knocked down to him.

"I got him a lot cheaper than I thought so I was pretty happy with the result. The little bugger played up when he was leaving the sale ring but I was real pleased with that because he kept showing that little bit of spirit that had sparked my interest in him in the first place."

Unbeknown to Mick, one of the under bidders was suffering from a respiratory infection and was forced to leave the complex to be attended to by medics; another bit of luck to go Mick's way. His luck at the sale wasn't all good. He also purchased a Tough Speed filly from a Rory's Jester mare, also bred by Armidale Stud. He paid only $4000 but she was subsequently given away as a pet. "The filly never made it to the races but she found a nice home where her slowness was appreciated."

The focus for Mick was always on the Savoire Vivre colt but his antics at Mick's Longford stables when he arrived after the sale gave the trainer his share of sleepless nights. Mick expected the colt to be flighty as was the case with many other young horses that had wandered into his yard, although he didn't have the luxury of small, fenced paddocks at Quarrel's property as he had at Alan Stubbs' complex, so he was forced to make do. A few days after Lot 3 arrived, his coltish behaviour became a problem.

"I was rapt that the colt showed character but there was only one way to put an end to his antics. I had to make him lighter so the vet was called in to take away his manhood. A bloody good job that we had it done. I reckon he would have been an absolute nightmare had he stayed a colt."

MIKAYLA Flack has worked alongside Mick for more than a decade and she was working for him when he bought The Cleaner. She also has a keen eye for a good horse so it came as no surprise when she told Mick what she thought of his yearling sale buy when he first landed at the stables.

"I had planned to go to the sale because Mick had been talking about this horse that he was keen to have a look at but I ended up staying at the stables that day. But when I arrived at work the next morning the horse was in a box and when he was walked out I could see straight away why Mick was so excited about getting him. He was a lovely moving animal and he had a bit of attitude about him too that I liked," Mikayla said.

Mikayla has been working with horses ever since she left school after completing year 10 at Kings Meadows High School in 1998. Her first job was as a stablehand at Alan Stubbs' stables when Mick was foreman. She was born in Longford and has been around horses all her life. She was raised on a farm and she still lives a farm life with her partner who manages a property in the Longford municipality. When she started out working in the racing industry she was relatively naïve but now in her early 30s, she is well versed in all aspects of the game.

NOT long after the sale Mick considered selling a couple of shares in the colt but the thought was short-lived. He then set about mapping out a budget to pay for the youngster. As had been the case in the past Magic Millions offered Mick time to settle up for his purchases, but no sooner had he worked out a payment plan he received a phone call that would have more far-reaching affects than he could have imagined.

"John Farrell called me to let me know that he had been diagnosed with cancer and that because it would be too difficult for him to travel north to see his horses on a regular basis, he wanted them sent to another trainer in Hobart. He owned a dozen of the 16 horses I had in work at the time, which effectively meant three-quarters of my stable had disappeared in one fell swoop. I didn't know what I was going to do."

The money he had planned to earn from training fees was to pay for his purchases, in particular Lot 3, as well as an array of other things Mick needed for the day-to-day running of his training operation. He was no stranger to bad news but this knocked him about so much that he was unable to sleep.

"I understood why John wanted his horses back so I just said 'okay mate' and made arrangements to have them sent down to Hobart. Owners change stables all the time and John (Farrell) genuinely wanted his horses moved so that he could see them more often. I understood that but all of a sudden I had only four horses in work and no other income. Unless I could find a truckload of new owners and fill up those boxes quickly, I was possibly going to lose my new youngsters. I couldn't go to the bank because money was tight and besides I was almost 60, and had no proper residence other than a two-room portable in a stable complex. It's fair to say it was the worst news I'd had since the call to tell me Lyn had died."

Mick tried everything he knew to find the cash to pay for the colt but his efforts came to nought, so he had to make the call to Magic Millions to let the company know of his predicament. The company agreed to give Mick more time to pay but told him that interest would accrue on the debt.

Meanwhile the now gelding was dispatched back to Armidale Stud where he was conceived and had spent the first 14 months of his life. He roamed the spelling paddocks for the remainder of the summer and first couple of months of autumn before being sent to the breakers. The breaking in process went smoothly although Mick had to have the breaker back a couple of times to rectify some minor issues.

Almost 18 months had passed when Mick asked a few of his golfing buddies, Bill Fawdry, Paul Burt, Jim Lowish and Alwyn "Ace" Shaw for help. The five would play every Tuesday or Wednesday, depending on each other's commitments and flog their way around the picturesque 18-hole layout at Prospect, a 15-minute drive from Launceston's CBD. They'd play for dollar-a-hole skins with jackpots, a couple of $5 nearest the pins with a winner-take-all pot of $50. They were all of similar ability so after a year they would all break even, although Mick liked to brag that he had their measure.

This day they'd played four holes when Mick revealed his problem. He was calm and cool as he told his buddies he needed to settle up and that they might be his last resort.

"I asked if they were interested in taking a quarter share each and they all said they'd think about it. After we finished the game Fawdry and Lowish said they were keen to be in it and Burt said he was keen but it would all depend on him selling one of the mining pumps he manufactured. Ace (Shaw) said he wasn't interested so I had two definite and one maybe.

"I told them that there had been interest accruing on the account with Magic Millions so the $10,000 sale price was probably going to be closer to $15,000. The kicker for me was that the deal was only on the table if I was to be the trainer."

Fawdry and Lowish agreed to take 25% each, and as luck would have it, Burt was able to sell his pump and agreed to take the remaining 50%. Mick had solved his problem and Magic Millions got their money. All Mick had to worry about now was teaching the youngster how to become a racehorse. One thing that will haunt Mick for the rest of his life was his failure to keep at least a 10 per cent share in the horse. "Not keeping a share in the colt is probably my biggest regret but the owners were great mates and I convinced myself that I was content just to be the trainer."

Many newcomers to the racing business take a lot of time and energy naming their new 'asset'. Not this time. Mick tells the story, with a glint in his eye.

"Paul Burt," he said, "had a cleaner come to his house a few days a week.

One morning he was sitting at his desk downstairs and as he glanced up to the top level his cleaning lady was standing at the top of the stairs and unbeknown to her she was, shall we say, a little exposed.

"At the time, he was putting together a list of possible names for the horse and he had the registration forms in front of him so he wrote down 'The Cleaner'."

The Cleaner was one of the ten names which had to provided to the registrar of the Stud Book and that's the one approved for the gelded son of Savoire Vivre.

15

Early Days

WHEN The Cleaner returned from the spelling paddock to tackle life as a racehorse he was a long way from being a ready made galloper. The feistiness had gone and he was behaving more like a lead pony. He seemed interested only in eating and sleeping but on the odd occasion during the learning process he would show Mick something that kept alive his faith in the gelding.

The horse also needed a stable name so Mick sized him up and reckoned he looked like a Bill, and it stuck.

"I knew it was going to be a slow, drawn out process to get him to the racetrack and thankfully the owners were prepared to be patient. He'd do something a bit special every time he came into work and he improved marginally each preparation and that improvement was enough to convince me he would eventually make a racehorse."

Mick persevered with restructuring the horse's training regime and slowly but surely the gelding started to respond. "When you've got one or two good horses in the stable it makes it easier to tackle the early morning starts but it takes a bloody good one to make you want to fire up in the winter. I had this eerie feeling that Bill was a good'un even though he was a lazy bastard who was more interested in eating and generally being a nuisance around the stables. It was the way he carried himself and he had this spark in his eyes that set him apart from any other horse in the stable. His stride was long so he covered a lot of ground as he walked and when he galloped it was even more pronounced and that was another thing I liked about him."

By the time Mick was ready to take The Cleaner to the trials he was developing into a handsome specimen and while his first public trial wasn't quite a disaster, he followed up with a trial win on his home track at Longford with local track rider David Quinn aboard. He came from back in the field of five to get up and edge out Go Hard Or Go Home, who was trained by his breeder Graeme McCulloch. At The Cleaner's first start, on February 10, 2011 he finished 13th of 14, in a 1200 metre maiden in Launceston more than 14 lengths from the winner (the rider was Rasit Yetimova, a fact that may assist some trivia players). At his second start he was a distant last of 10, a fortnight later, beaten about 11 lengths. He never got warm in either run, so Mick pulled the pin and started again.

"He was just being a prick and would play games when he went to the races. His trackwork had been good but for whatever reason he just refused to take that work into his races. He was developing into a lovely looking animal and I was sure all I had to do was work out how to get the stupidity out of him.

"It wasn't that he was a dumb horse it was just that he didn't understand what it was he was meant to do and that sometimes only gets fixed with age. So I kept telling the owners he needed more time. Thankfully they didn't have to wait too long for a bit of joy.

"I gave him a freshen-up after his second start and when I took him back to the trials about three months later he won a trial and beat home a very good horse in Spy Wears Prado, trained by Dianne Ray-Luttrell. I knew then I was on the right track. He was still being a bit of a prick on the training track but I was prepared to put up with his shit because he was showing other good signs."

BEING bred along staying lines there was every chance The Cleaner would not excel until he stepped out over a decent amount of ground. After the freshen-up Mick sent him around in a 1400-metre maiden at Launceston; he finished 8th of 14 but he was only three lengths from the winner. Cameron Quilty rode him but he was far from enthused with the effort. Quilty was on at his next start, at Hobart over 1600 metres, and after being beaten four lengths the rider's thoughts left Mick shaking his head.

"Quilty told me I'd be better off moving the horse on because he didn't think he'd amount to much. I guess on face value he was entitled to that opinion but he didn't know what I knew, so I just ignored him."

That night Mick was scratching his head trying to work out who he could get to ride The Cleaner at his first try over 2100 metres. A young fellow from Mauritius named Jacques Luxe had lobbed in Tasmania to further his career in the care of talented trainer Vicki Rhind. Mick liked what he'd seen of the mature-age apprentice who was able to claim the new maximum of four kilograms, so he called Rhind to firm up the booking.

Luxe was 25 when he landed in Australia having had only seven race rides in Mauritius and headed firstly to the stables of top Sydney trainer David Payne. When that didn't work out he moved south to Melbourne and to the stables of Mick Price. Luxe worked hard so Price allowed him to ride trackwork and after three years the trainer took him on as an apprentice.

Price eventually suggested he go to Tasmania because he believed he might get more opportunities to ride in races, a story for so many riders in the past, including Stephen Maskiell who went on to dominate Tasmania's jockey ranks, eventually making his way into the Tasmanian Racing Hall of Fame.

On June 26, 2011, The Cleaner lined up in a maiden/class one over the 2100 metres at Launceston, and Mick was fired up. He'd been promising his golfing mates that all the horse needed was more ground and this was to be something of an acid test for both horse and trainer.

The Cleaner looked sharp but with only two runs under his belt Mick wasn't completely sure it was enough to see him through his first test beyond 1600 metres. The Cleaner now stood tall at just beyond 16 hands and Mick had managed his muscular development superbly. All that remained was to see if the horse had the ability to match his physique.

"I wasn't sure we had ourselves a good horse because there was still every chance he was a pretender. They're the horses that show up when there's no real pressure on them but when it gets serious they throw in the towel. I was keen to get him over 2100 metres so I had Stephen Maskiell ride the horse for me in work and he told me to put him over the longer trip, whack a set of blinkers on him and get him to lead and that should get him going because he reckoned he wasn't comfortable with other horses around him."

It was D-Day for trainer and horse and Luxe listened intently to Mick's every word before mounting up. Mick had taken Maskiell's suggestion on board, and when he legged up his jockey he told him to dash The Cleaner out of the gates and to make sure he rated the horse well in front. The Cleaner led comfortably and seemed to relish the role of pacemaker but at the 600-metre peg Luxe looked to be struggling to steer the horse as The Cleaner wobbled around the bend. In the straight he looked like a drunk as he wandered from one side of the track to the other over the final 300 metres. Mick couldn't understand why he'd been so erratic in the home straight. The Cleaner finished second, beaten 4-1/2 lengths by Master Joseph. The winner was prepared by Larry Dalco, one of the mentors who had helped Mick when he was first starting out as a trainer.

The owners had all backed their potential stayer in from $34 to $19 with the place portion of their each-way bets netting them all a healthy profit. When Luxe dismounted he praised The Cleaner's effort but said he couldn't explain why the horse had been so hard to steer, especially in the home straight when he was calling on him for a big effort.

Mick remained baffled for but a few minutes, but when he took off the bridle a tooth fell out. Obviously it had been disengaged during the race and had been caught in the ring piece of the bit. The Cleaner had run his race with a tooth dislodged. The bit gouging into an exposed hole in his mouth had no doubt caused him pain.

"I couldn't believe it when the tooth dropped out. There wasn't much blood in his mouth but there's no doubt the tooth becoming dislodged would have been what caused him to wander all over the place. The poor bugger must have been wondering what was going on and the rider would have been oblivious to it. I gave him a few days to recover and everything was back to normal within a week."

Armed with a bit more confidence Mick entered The Cleaner four weeks later in a maiden/class one, also at Launceston, this time over 2150 metres. He added blinkers, booked Luxe to ride and told the owners to have a decent bet.

Telling one of the owners, Paul Burt, to 'have a bet' is like unleashing a guard dog on a home invader. The plunge was aggressive with The Cleaner backed in from $6 to start the $2.70 favourite. Luxe's claim had been reduced to three kilograms owing to him having won five races in Tasmania since his previous ride on The Cleaner but the horse would still carry only 53kg. 'Bill' looked in great fettle as he paraded before the race, so much so that Burt decided to have another crack on the Tote when he saw the gelding's price drift out to $3.

"The instructions were to lead, the same as before and the kid had no trouble doing that because he struggled to hold him but he managed to rein him in a bit and set a good tempo and when he let him go at the top of the straight he just left 'em for dead. He got a bit tired at the end but that was understandable given it was only his second try at the distance. Leading and having a bit left to fight it out at the finish is no mean feat for a maiden horse." He ended up winning by more than three lengths. The Cleaner was on his way.

AT last Mick and his golfing mates had something to smile about. Fawdry looked like the proverbial Cheshire Cat while Burt rushed down to the mounting yard to applaud the first horse he had ever owned as he returned to the winner's stall for the first time. On the way he was checking all of his pockets for the multitude of Tote and bookies' tickets that would soon be turned into wads of cash. Lowish was more subdued but there was no confusion in his body language as he listened intently to what Luxe had to say when he dismounted.

The Cleaner clearly relished the new riding tactics. He won at his next two starts over 2100 metres, at short odds, in Launceston before Mick took him to Devonport to race on the synthetic all-weather track that had proved to be the saviour for the Devonport Racing Club. The club had been fading on the vine owing to a sub-standard turf racing surface that caused meetings to be rained out more often than not during the winter months.

About $10 million had been invested on the all-weather project and although there were a few teething problems in the first year the success of the investment is best measured by the amount of wagering turnover on Devonport meetings today that has it rivalling that of the two grass track venues in Hobart and Launceston. The project had been underwritten by the Tasmanian Government that agreed with the governing body, Tasracing, that the state needed an all weather track so that winter cancellations elsewhere could be avoided.

Mick was naturally anxious the first time The Cleaner stepped foot on the all-weather Tapeta surface. Tapeta is a patented blend of wax-coated sand, rubber and fibre and is impervious to weather, never turns to mud, gives very little kick back, and holds up under varied and severe weather conditions and is mostly fast and dry.

The track was still going through a settling in period and while most trainers raved about it there were a couple of sceptics who preferred to highlight the negatives. But what would racing be without those doubting Thomases?

Mick wasn't sure how the horse would handle the synthetic but if he was going to have a crack at a Devonport Cup later in the year he needed to find out in the lower grade. There were reports that some horses couldn't go a yard on the Tapeta surface and that played on Mick's mind on the trip from Longford. But he could have saved himself the worry because Luxe urged The Cleaner from the gates and the end result was never in doubt with The Cleaner, at $1.70, going on to win by 2-1/2 lengths without being fully extended. But the most pleasing aspect was that he smashed the 1880-metre track record clocking 1m.59.66 over the Devonport Cup trip.

"I was stoked when he won like he did. It was his first look at Devonport and I pretty much thought that all I had to do was have the horse right on the day and the Cup would be his for the taking. He'd now won four in a row and everyone was starting to see what I saw in him when I first laid eyes on him. We were all pretty chuffed about how he was racing and we were looking forward to the Devonport Cup."

The Cleaner had his colours lowered at his next start over 2100 metres in Hobart but he was second ($3.20 fav.) to Norsqui, a horse trained by veteran mentor Walter McShane who also had eyes on bigger prizes with his horse. Norsqui would go on and win the Mornington Cup a few months later before finishing a game third in the Group 2 Adelaide Cup over 3200 metres.

Norsqui retuned to Morphettville the next season to win the Adelaide Cup and two starts later almost landed an incredible double when he finished less than a length short of winning the Group 1 Sydney Cup over the same trip.

Mick gave The Cleaner a couple of weeks off to freshen him up for what promised to be an interesting and hopefully profitable campaign that would take in all the major local cups starting with the big one in Devonport in early January.

Mick started The Cleaner's next campaign off in a benchmark 78 over 2100 metres under lights in Launceston on November 23, and while he was run down by Prevailing, who would go on and win the Launceston Cup that season, Mick wasn't fazed because he knew his stable star was in need of the run. Three weeks later Mick sought the services of Stephen Maskiell to guide The Cleaner at his first start in open company. The Brighton Cup has long been a lead-up race for the Devonport Cup and Hobart Cup and Mick wanted to make sure his front-running machine was on track to tackle each of those races.

Both horse and rider delivered everything that was expected with The Cleaner turning the tables on the $2 favourite. Prevailing, winning by more than three lengths. It was also another successful betting venture for the owners backed their charge from $5 into $3.70. Mick also let the moths out of his wallet and uncharacteristically, at least at this stage of his life, unloaded.

WHEN The Cleaner was on one of his winning streaks Mick was always an easy target for his children, as far as money was concerned.

"I'd probably go months without seeing any of the kids but when The Cleaner won a decent race I knew I'd have some regular visits in the coming weeks but I was just pleased to see my kids and I felt good to be able to give them a few bucks," Mick said.

Carissa looked at the success Mick had with The Cleaner from a different perspective. "Horses have always kept Dad broke and that's just something that's never going to change. The Cleaner gave him money for a while but we all knew that once the horse stopped racing it would be back to normal for Dad. When Mum and Dad were together and getting along without drink or gambling it was Mum who always had a backup plan and that was to try and have some money put aside in case of emergency while Dad would just live for the day," she said.

16

Onwards & Upwards

BY now The Cleaner had won his way into the hearts of the purists who fully appreciated the enormity of him being able to do all the bullocking work in front and then have the stamina to stave off any challengers at the business end of a race. Mick still had no idea that his stable star wasn't far away from taking his trainer on the ride of a lifetime. His win in the Brighton Cup, at his first test at open company, had Mick and the owners cock-a-hoop about the prospects of tackling the major Tassie cups. The Cleaner had delivered exactly what Mick had predicted and when he emerged from his box the next morning the trainer was even more enthused.

"After he won the Brighton Cup his manners had changed. I don't know exactly what it was but he was different after he won that race. At home at the stables he walked around as if he owned the joint and even the trackwork riders and stable hands said he felt different, but in a positive way. I'm sure horses know when they're winners, especially Bill. After each win he got cocky and became a bit aloof, like a cat, but it only lasted a day and then he'd be back to normal."

The bond between a man and his horse isn't often likened to that of man and his dog but in the case of Mick and Bill it rang true because the horse was now starting to respond to his trainer's voice.

"I reckon he'd been racing for a year when he started to do things that no other horse had ever done with me. He would follow me around the paddock and play with me. I'd make a move like I was going to chase him and he'd almost crouch forward and then he'd dart off in the opposite direction, just like a dog. There were heaps of things we'd do when he was in his little paddock behind the stables that would keep us amused for hours.

"It got to the stage where I didn't really have to put a lead rope on him because he would just follow me wherever I wanted him to go. One day I was walking down the run to the paddock to tend to another horse and he was walking behind me and I stopped, turned around and I told him to get in his box and he stopped, thought for a second and then walked into his box. It was probably one of the most magical moments in my life to have a horse respond to me in that way but that was how we were.

"I'd be taking a bit of a breather leaning up against a fence post and he'd sidle up behind me and hang his head over my shoulder. He'd just stay there for ages and wouldn't move until I told him to piss off—he knew what that meant too. He was a horse who had a set routine that he'd stick to. He'd go to the same spot in a paddock to have a sleep or to have a roll and when he felt a bit frisky he'd go lairising around the paddock but he'd always pull up at the same spot on the fence line. When he strolled around the paddock he had a certain swagger about him that was kind of majestic. Im sure he knew he was very good.

"The other thing I love about The Cleaner is his nature. He hasn't got a mean bone in his body. I never had to walk from side to side to do up the leg straps on his rug. I'd just walk underneath him and there have been kids who have done the same. He's got such a kind nature. He was an absolute pleasure to have around the stables but he didn't like being taken out of his comfort zone. He likes things to be routine and whenever you changed something, whether it be in his work or to move something around at the stable he would get a bit unsettled. He is a creature of habit. We are all a bit like that really."

MIKAYLA Flack could see the way the pair were bonding: "I pretty much know what makes Mick tick because I've been around him long enough. He really loves his horses and that's probably why he was able to get the best out of The Cleaner. Mick's horse smart and I've learned a hell of a lot from him over the years. The things I saw with him and The Cleaner I've never seen with any other horse and trainer.

'Bill' would pretty much do whatever Mick told him to, within reason. The horse would follow Mick around like a bad smell and I'd often catch them sharing a moment in the back paddock. It was good to see that because Mick hasn't had the best of health these past few years and The Cleaner was probably the main thing that was keeping him going."

Mikayla had a crack at training a few years ago. She took out an owner-trainer licence and had a couple of boxes at Longford but she never tasted the joy of winning a race.

"I have been around horses long enough to know what it takes to train one and that's why I gave it a shot with a couple of horses a while back but it's not as easy as you first think so I ended up not renewing my licence after a couple of years. I haven't given up hope of doing it again but it's got to be when the time's right and that could be tomorrow or in five years. We'll just have to wait and see. Maybe I'll form a partnership with Mick. Now that would be interesting."

MICK believed Bill still needed another run before he tackled the Devonport Cup so he turned his attention to the Longford Cup on New Year's Day, 2012. He knew the handicapper would probably give The Cleaner 57kg, given he'd just won the Brighton Cup. He put Luxe back on top so the horse would only have to lug 55kg (his claim was now down to two kilos). The Cleaner, at $1.80, scooted around his home track covering the 1800 metres in 1.49.20 to win by more than four lengths from the David and Scott Brunton-trained Lightly Spiced with a bunch of battlers trailing out behind. The Longford Cup carried prizemoney of $15,500 but it was a hometown cup and pushed all the right buttons for Mick and the owners.

The Devonport Cup, worth $100,000 ($60,000 to the winner), was just 10 days away. The Cleaner had emerged from the Longford Cup in top order and the boys were starting to dream of how they might celebrate a Devonport Cup win. The Cleaner had been assigned the minimum of 54kg, he held the 1880m track record and he was in better form than when he had set the record four months earlier. Punters rallied for The Cleaner as his odds tumbled in from $4 to $3.20. Most of the racing scribes were claiming a slight bias to frontrunners in earlier races and predicted that would give The Cleaner an unbeatable edge; but racing has a habit of making fools of geniuses.

Stephen Maskiell, the multiple premiership-winning rider, was given the responsibility of piloting the popular elect. The Cleaner looked a picture in the mounting yard and when he sprang into stride for the preliminary warm-up he had his neck arched and even gave a little squeal as he headed towards the starting stalls. When the gates opened he was quickly into stride and had no trouble finding the lead but as the field approached the home turn it was evident he was in a bit of strife as Mr Isaac, a $41 chance from the Gary White stable, collared the leader with a stack of contenders making their moves.

It was the Troy Blacker-trained Dream Flyer who emerged from the pack and hit the line a length clear of Catwen Boy and the Tony McEvoy-trained Uchimura, the only interstate invader in the field of 13. The Cleaner finished seventh, but was a well beaten 6-1/2 lengths from the winner.

"It was hard to know what to make of that run because there's no doubt the horse was in top order but when Steve came back he said he wasn't the same horse who had won the Brighton Cup just a month earlier.

I checked the horse over and his legs seemed fine, his heart rate was good and he appeared bright after the race. At first I thought he might have had an off day, after all we are talking about horses and if there's one thing I've learned over the years it's to never count your chickens."

The following day Mick found his stable star was favouring his nearside front leg. A subsequent vet's inspection and X-rays revealed a couple of small bone chips in the horse's nearside front fetlock joint. Keyhole surgery was performed by top Longford-based veterinarian Mike Morris who extracted the chips with little fuss and The Cleaner was then sent for a well-earned spell while Mick mapped out a winter campaign for the rising five-year-old.

17

Crossing Bass Strait

THE Cleaner resumed in the winter of 2012 with two consecutive wins in Hobart, both on wet ground. Both were in open company—the first over 1600m and the next over his pet distance of 2100m—with underrated jockey Shannon Brazil aboard.

Brazil had relocated from Victoria to Tasmania three years earlier to try and establish her career in the saddle, having spent a couple of seasons riding on King Island to gain regular race riding experience as she was struggling to secure opportunities in her home state.

But riding trackwork in Longford gave her an opportunity to link up with Mick's stable and for her hard work and enthusiasm she was rewarded with two rides on Tasmania's new star. Mick had begun thinking about an interstate trip and if the horse emerged from his first two outings without a hitch he would target two or three races in Victoria, and then bring him home to prepare for another summer campaign in Tasmania.

Mick pencilled in a race at Moonee Valley over the Cox Plate distance (2040m) in the first week of the new racing season. To give him every chance of securing his first interstate winner he booked the services of star Tasmanian-born jockey Craig Newitt, who was only too pleased to accommodate.

Newitt has known Mick most of his life and regards him as a smart trainer who has a genuine love and understanding of horses. When Newitt was apprenticed to Tasmania's master of apprentices Leon Wells, Mick always offered an ear for the then youngster, who, as a teenager, was taking the racing industry by storm in his home state. Newitt has continued to dominate in top level racing across the nation and while he endured a rough patch early in his career after a falling out with stewards he has emerged a stronger person for the experience; there isn't a more professional rider in Australia.

"Mick's a great bloke. I have known him since I was a little kid," Newitt said. "I remember plenty of conversations we had as I was growing up so when he called me to ride The Cleaner at his first start in Victoria I never even bothered to check if I had anything else pencilled in for the race.

"The amazing thing about The Cleaner is that Mick called me about six months before the horse had started and he told me that he was pretty sure he had the best horse that he's ever likely to train in his yard and he was talking about The Cleaner. I watched the horse's first two starts and I thought to myself—you poor bastard—the horse struggled to beat the ambulance home and I felt so sorry for Mick. But he had faith in the horse and it's an absolute credit to a bloke who has worked his arse off all his life with the hope of getting a horse that might win him Group races."

The Cleaner lined up in an open handicap at Moonee Valley, a very winnable race. Punters thought so too, as he opened and closed at $4.20. Also entered was another Tasmanian horse, the $3.10 favourite, Banca Mo, who would eventually burst on the national scene later in the season. The Cleaner led as was expected and he was travelling well within himself to the home turn but bobbing along close-up was Banca Mo, a last start winner at Flemington. When talented apprentice Ben Knobel gave his charge a touch more rein Banca Mo cruised to the lead and hit the line with three lengths to spare over The Cleaner. Banca Mo was to have one more start in that preparation before being tipped out for a spell.

Mick and The Cleaner's owners took the defeat on the chin and while winning would have been a great result, the second prizemoney of $18,000 was more than he had received for any of his eight wins in Tasmania. They also conceded they may have been beaten by a very good horse—and they would be proven right. Banca Mo, who would win Cups at Pakenham, Warrnambool and Mornington, and $812,000 in prizemoney, had cost only $2100 at the same Tasmanian yearling sale as The Cleaner. Mick was hoping his bargain buy would one day emulate the feats of Banca Mo. Deep down he was hoping for more.

MICK was encouraged by The Cleaner's first try on the mainland so he set him for a $35,000 race at Sandown a few weeks later and booked Knobel for the ride. It was a benchmark 0-89 race over 2100 metres with only six in the field so to say it was a walk in the park would be an understatement. The Cleaner won by just under two lengths but the way he won made a statement and sparked some interest from the media who immediately likened the Tasmanian to the bold frontrunner Vo Rogue who had made his mark in the late 1980s showing the same up front courage and tenacity to break his rivals.

This was the start of a journey that would take Mick on the ride of his life. He still didn't know exactly what he had in his grasp but each time The Cleaner stepped out he'd show Mick something extra and that was what gave the trainer a feeling that he might truely have something special, that his earliest instincts were right on the money. One more outing ended The Cleaner's first interstate campaign and while he could only manage a fifth of 11 behind Dame Claire in the Listed Ansett Stakes over 2400m at Mornington, Mick was proud of what the horse had achieved at his first try on the mainland.

"There were a few knockers who said I was just trying to chase a dream but I knew I had something special and these first few trips away were just to get the horse used to travelling and he handled it really well. I took him back and forth by boat and he was happy with the whole deal." That deal was pure Mick.

"My mate Vern Poke has a horse transport business and he gave Bill some special treatment but after the first trip you would have thought the horse had been doing it all his life. He'd get on the truck at the stables in Longford and we'd head to Devonport, get the horse off at Vern's place at Quoiba, near the ferry terminal, where he'd have a roll and a pick and then hop back on the truck for the trip across the water. Vern recommended that we stay at a place called Pine Lodge at Oaklands Junction and it was perfect for what we wanted."

Pine Lodge Stud is a harness racing stud farm located about 10 minutes' drive north of Melbourne's Tullamarine Airport. Its rolling hills and well laid out yards surround a well maintained 600-metre training track.

"Vern said he was sure I'd like the place and that it would be perfect for Bill and he was spot on. As soon as we got there I'd walk the horse a couple of laps of the track and then he'd go into a walk-in walk-out yard, just like the one at home, so the horse felt right at home from the get go.

"As long as he knew I was there everything was sweet. We'd rarely stay overnight though. I much preferred to bring him home straight after the races but if we were in a very late race and time wouldn't allow us to make the return trip deadline, we'd stay the extra day but the least amount of time we had to spend in Melbourne the better."

The Cleaner had a couple of weeks off after the Mornington run but he never left Mick's stable. Mick knew the horse well so a couple of weeks just loafing around the paddock and spending half-hour stints picking on some lush grass at the stables was enough of a break for the horse to recover from each campaign. Mick had his eyes on another crack at the Devonport Cup and he planned on giving The Cleaner a trial and then one start before taking him back to Devonport for the Cup. At the last minute he had a rethink and instead of giving him a trial he entered him in the Listed weight-for-age Tasmanian Stakes over 1600 metres in Hobart on December 12.

"I thought we'd might as well run in the weight-for-age race because I knew it wouldn't be a big field and it was worth $54,000 to the winner. I knew the horse was fit enough to cope with a first-up run over a mile and I figured that the horses nominated for the race wouldn't be as fit as my bloke.

"I put Jason Maskiell on because he was back in the game after messing up over in Melbourne and he was keen to do the right thing. We had a fit horse and a jockey who'd be trying hard to win. I reckoned that was a good combination."

Maskiell was dubbed the whiz kid from Longford and was being hailed the next best thing to come out of Tasmania when he climbed his way up the jockeys' premiership table in Victoria riding Group and Listed winners and matching it with the likes of Damien Oliver and Craig Williams during the 2011-12 season.

But with money to burn and the sudden urge to live life in the fast lane, Jason started mixing with the wrong crowd in Melbourne and slowly but surely his career slid down the gurgler. Testing positive to the drug ice led to a six-month ban in 2011.

"A lot of people make decisions in their lives that they are not proud of," Maskiell said, "and mine was to get involved with drugs. I had everything going for me but I just got in with the wrong crowd and one thing led to another and before I knew it I had a problem and it has been a real battle to get clean."

Mick and the owners of The Cleaner wanted to give Maskiell a chance to reboot his career and to the kid's credit he worked hard to stay clear of the problem—for a while. Maskiell delivered the goods at his first ride on The Cleaner and the owners made sure they let the rider know how pleased they were to have him on board.

Mick couldn't get the smile off his face when Maskiell brought The Cleaner back to the enclosure. Not only was his strategy endorsed but his horse had just beaten home the $1.70 favourite Geegees Blackflash. The Cleaner simply toyed with his opposition, beating the favourite by four lengths, and Mick left the course that night convinced his special horse was about to blossom.

The Cleaner ventured to Launceston for his next start under lights in a quality handicap over 1600 metres and it was the same result, although this time Geegees Blackflash went within a length of turning the tables, and it was the Cleaner who was odds on ($1.60), with a 4.5 kilo weight advantage over his rival.

The Cleaner was on a roll and Mick told the owners that all their horse needed to do was show up at Devonport the following week and the Devonport Cup was his for the taking. Punters rallied for the bold front-runner who started the $2.60 favourite but again Bill failed to flatter and this time he finished a dismal 10th of 14 with the Patrick Payne-trained Fieldmaster proving too good for Lightly Spiced and Jakcorijim. Maskiell dismounted and shook his head in disbelief as Mick rushed to check the horse's legs for fear he had suffered an injury, but everything looked in order and then the rider explained how the horse felt in the run.

"He was gone at the winning post the first time," Maskiell said. "He was off the bit all the way and just couldn't get going. I didn't know what to think but there was one thing for sure he wasn't the horse I'd ridden at his two previous starts."

WITH another Devonport Cup behind them, Mick was now convinced his star did not handle the synthetic and he focused on the two major Tasmanian Cups still to come. Although he knew The Cleaner wasn't a genuine 2400-metre horse he was confident he would make his presence felt and he looked to his next start in the 2100m Summer Cup at Hobart on January 20, that would tell him if the horse was in good enough shape to tackle the G3 Hobart Cup over the 2400 metres. With young Maskiell back on top the gelding toughed it out to defeat Norsqui by a half-length with Fieldmaster two lengths in third, but it was the way The Cleaner refused to wilt over the final 200 metres that impressed Mick and convinced him the horse was ready for a crack at the big Cup.

"You never know for sure how a horse is going to perform after it puts in a shocker and we were no different with Bill, but he let us know, in no uncertain terms, how he was feeling. He probably had a bit up his sleeve on the line and there were some good ones that finished behind him including Norsqui and Geegees Blackflash. It was a ripper effort, so it was all systems go for the Cup. I had two weeks to get him ready and I knew it wouldn't take much work to get him spot on for the race. My only query was whether he'd run out a strong 2400 metres."

By now The Cleaner and Geegees Blackflash, from the John Luttrell stable, were becoming arch rivals. Both horses had a huge following, especially Blackflash who had shown more versatility than any other horse in the modern era in Tasmania. He could sprint brilliantly early in his prep to win feature races over 1200 metres, including the state's most prestigious sprint event, the Newmarket Handicap, and his efforts at 1600 metres were just as impressive; but he could also stay and that is what set him apart from the rest. After winning the 2011 Newmarket as a four-year-old, Geegees Blackflash went on to win the 2012 Hobart Cup over 2400 metres. He would then run a luckless second in the Launceston Cup behind Prevailing, beaten in a photo finish, after which his rider Peter Mertens admitted he had pulled the trigger too early. The narrow defeat had cost the champ a place in history as one of an elite group to have won both major cups in the same season.

Mick stayed focused and when The Cleaner delivered a brilliant track gallop four days out from the Cup it instilled even more confidence within the camp.

"I was fairly confident going into the 2013 Hobart Cup because the horse's trackwork the week before the race was probably the best he'd shown me in his career. I had to change his work around slightly because he was going to 2400 metres so I just upped the tempo of his pace work for that fortnight and after his gallop the week of the Cup I told the owners it would take a really good horse to beat him."

The media hype around the Hobart Cup that year focused on The

Cleaner and Geegees Blackflash. Having two horses of that calibre, along with five interstate invaders from some of the best stables (Gai Waterhouse, Darren Weir, Robert Smerdon, Tony Vasil and Patrick Payne had starters), ensured plenty of pre-race publicity. Weir was aiming to win his fourth Hobart Cup, having already won with True Courser (2006), Offenbach (2008) and Gotta Keep Cool (2009).

Weir had set Hurdy Gurdy Man for the race three months earlier. Tasmanians are a fickle lot when it comes to feature races, especially when the big guns lob from the mainland, which is why Hurdy Gurdy Man started $3.80 favourite with Norsqui second pick at $6.90 the best-backed of the locals. Geegees Blackflash blew like the north wind in the betting, easing to $9.50, while The Cleaner's price drifted to $8 before firming slightly to start at $7.30.

Mick and The Cleaner's owners had formed a pact to dress up for each feature race by sporting outfits that matched Mick's racing colours of black with sky blue epaulettes and sleeves, black armbands and sky blue cap, so they all donned a black suit, black shirt and a sky blue tie. It looked impressive and added to the theatre every time The Cleaner tackled a Group or Listed race.

When the gates crashed back Maskiell had to work on The Cleaner to get him across from his wide gate (11) in the field of 15 but with a long run to the first turn he had no trouble finding the rail with Norsqui camped just off the speed and Waterhouse's charge Power Broker on The Cleaner's back, as planned. Mertens had Geegees Blackflash in a good spot midfield with Hurdy Gurdy Man neatly tucked away on the fence worse than midfield with his rider Glen Boss happy to have his charge doing little work.

Young Maskiell was rating The Cleaner perfectly but when he lifted the tempo 700 metres out Mertens was awake to his tactics and set Geegees Blackflash alight and when the pair locked horns at the top of the home straight the huge crowd cheered as the two local heroes settled down to stage what looked for certain to be a two-horse war. The Cleaner answered the first challenge and was holding Geegees Blackflash at bay and Maskiell was starting to think about what he might say at the presentation ceremony but Boss had extricated Hurdy Gurdy Man from the rails and was weaving his way through needle-eye openings.

The Cleaner was giving his all, as was Geegees Blackflash and 200 metres out Mick and his golfing mates were at full voice cheering home their champ, but Weir's lightweight hope found that extra something that only good horses find to go on and defeat The Cleaner by just over a length with Geegees Blackflash a half-head away third.

Instead of feeling deflated, Mick and the owners gathered at the runners up stall to greet their brave warrior. Even though Hurdy Gurdy Man had won the race, you would have thought it was The Cleaner or Geegees Blackflash who had emerged triumphant, so loud were the cheers and applause for the Tassie pair as they strolled along the pathway leading to the enclosure.

"I was so proud of the horse because he gave his all and in this game you can never ask for any more," said Mick. "Weir's a bloody good trainer and full credit to the bloke because he was smart enough to target a race that was going to get his horse in on the minimum weight (54 kg) and that's what he'd done with his previous three winners. It was a winning formula and he was able to identify the right horse for the race each time. Good on him."

The Cleaner had nowproven he could handle the 2400-metre trip so his growing band of followers sent him around the second elect at $4.50 in the Launceston Cup two weeks later. Hurdy Gurdy Man was the clear favourite at $3.70, but Geegees Blackflash fans were happy to take the $11 on offer and he was in to $8 by starting time. The Tony Vasil-trained Lucky Angel, with Craig Newitt aboard, firmed to start the $6.40 third favourite. A Lucky Angel victory would go close to breaking one on-course bookie.

With a natural pacemaker assured many of the well-fancied runners jostled for positions behind The Cleaner but it was to be a race of sensations with Hurdy Gurdy Man an early casualty. Weir's horse suffered a bleeding attack at the halfway mark and was pulled up, leaving his supporters gob-smacked.

All eyes were now focused on The Cleaner as he made play in front carrying a steadying 57.5 kilos. Geegees Blackflash, carrying topweight of 59.5 kilos, had travelled well for Mertens and with the memory of losing the race the previous year when he went too early, the talented rider had the big black horse poised to pounce as they wheeled into the home turn. When Mertens pushed the go button Geegees Blackflash unleashed his customary sprint and he hit the line two lengths clear of Lucky Angel with the Troy Blacker-trained Dream Pedlar almost four lengths away third. The Cleaner lobbed in seventh spot but was almost nine lengths from the winner.

The winning owners and the trainer struggled to hold back the tears as Mertens brought Geegees Blackflash back to the enclosure. The horse now had both major cups in the owners' trophy cabinet and at five years of age he had at least two more years left in him to continue to dominate in his home state.

Mick applauded the winner's effort but he was also sure The Cleaner would have bigger fish to fry after a spell. The bookie who had laid Lucky Angel to lose way more than he had in his bag or his bank account was seen hyperventilating into a brown paper bag for a good while after the race.

18

Changing Stables

THERE were plans to take The Cleaner to Melbourne for a few races during the winter leading to some heated exchanges between the trainer and the owners. The owners revealed they wanted to transfer the horse to Caulfield trainer Robert Smerdon.

Bill Fawdry had travelled to Melbourne a month earlier to check out Smerdon's training complex before making a decision to send the horse to him. Fawdry then encouraged the other two owners, Paul Burt and Jim Lowish, to go to Melbourne to see for themselves, and after the three of them had spent an afternoon with Smerdon the deal was done. Fawdry also made inquiries with Peter Moody but he wasn't impressed with his comments about The Cleaner.

"I talked to Peter Moody about training the horse and he said that he would not be comfortable taking on a horse that might win a race at Ararat and then have to send him back to Tasmania because he wasn't good enough to win another race, so needless to say the conversation went no further," Fawdry said.

This was the owners' first sign of their lack of faith in Mick. While he had to accept their decision, despite their agreement when the shares were allocated—that he would be the trainer—Mick didn't have to like it. He argued that at least they should allow him to take the horse to Melbourne for his first start of the campaign and then transfer him to Smerdon. Mick's reasoning was clearly driven by pride, but also by what he had achieved. The owners believed it made sense to give the horse the chance to contest major races in Victoria without the added pressure and expense of travelling to and from Tasmania for each of four or five starts, which became a costly exercise.

Mick was delighted when the owners agreed to his wishes and The Cleaner did his part with a stellar first-up performance to easily win the $101,500 ($62,500 first prize) David Bourke Provincial Plate over 1610 metres at Flemington with Jason Maskiell aboard.

"We were standing next to Robert (Smerdon) when The Cleaner was about to run in that first-up race at Flemington," said Fawdry, "and he kept telling me that the horse couldn't win because he'd drawn barrier 14 and there was too much early speed in the race, so we shouldn't be disappointed if he didn't run a place. But when we won he was amazed. He said that his first thought was that the horse could probably win a couple of Saturday grade races but after that effort he might win a Melbourne Cup!"

The Cleaner must have wondered what was going on when he was loaded onto a strange truck and transported to his new digs and without his mate by his side. There would be no more playful romps in the paddock he called his own and he would surely miss the regular hugs and general pampering from the only person who had ever shown him affection.

When Mick returned to Tasmania he was shaky but not shattered. He wanted The Cleaner to do well in Smerdon's care because he was confident in the horse's ability, but deep down he had a feeling that the horse would not take kindly to the hustle and bustle of a high profile big city stable environment.

The Cleaner had his first start for Smerdon two weeks later in the

Listed Winter Championship final over his pet distance of 1600m at Flemington. He was lumbered with top weight of 60 kilograms and again drew wide at 11. But neither of those elements had anything to do with his dismal performance. He finished second last and was beaten more than a dozen lengths. Craig Newitt partnered the horse that day and he too was dumbfounded and could offer no reasonable excuse why the horse had performed so poorly.

Maskiell was back on for his next start at Flemington in the Gala Supreme Handicap over 2000 metres, a race named in honour of the 1973 Melbourne Cup winner. A fifth of 14 was a better result and next start he ventured to Moonee Valley for a third of eight in a $100,000 handicap over the Cox Plate trip (2040m) with three kilogram-claiming apprentice Brodie Loy in the saddle. Smerdon waited four weeks before The Cleaner had his fourth start for the stable. The Listed Heatherlie Handicap over 1700 metres at Caulfield looked a suitable assignment but The Cleaner had never raced at the track, and he eased in the market from $10 to $16.

With Maskiell back on top after serving out a suspension the owners were expecting a good result but again The Cleaner raced sourly and was the first horse beaten turning for home. Mick had watched the race at home

"When I saw him in the mounting yard I rang Bill Fawdry and told him that if he didn't send the horse home straight away he wouldn't have a horse at all. I was fuming because the horse looked as though he'd dropped at least 60 kilos. I know the horse fretted. It's just the way he is. When a man and a horse spend as much time together as we did you can't help but form a bond."

Fawdry agreed with Mick and three days later The Cleaner was on the boat bound for Devonport. The horse looked relaxed when he stepped off the truck at Mick's stables and Mick could almost see the relief in the horse's eyes as Bill gave him a confronting nudge that almost knocked Mick off his feet, as if to say 'what did you do to me you old bastard'.

"The horse just didn't handle being boxed all the time and I'm sure his workload was way beyond what he'd been used to and that's in no way blaming anyone. It was just a matter of the horse being out of place in that environment. Anyway I was glad to have him back and it didn't take me long to get him into shape. I was keen to get him ready for a first-up tilt at the Newmarket in Launceston on November 20, after a three-month break, but it would all depend on him coming good but after I gave him a gallop about four weeks before the race I knew I had him back."

19

Home Again

THE Newmarket is a Quality Handicap, considered the most prestigious of Tasmania's 1200-metre sprints. It has been won by some of the greats of the state, including Geegees Blackflash (2011) and Mick was hoping his stable star could mirror that feat. With no more talk of taking the horse off Mick, he started mapping out a program that would include another shot at the Hobart Cup.

"I was unhappy when the horse was given to Smerdon to train but I must admit the exercise of leaving him over there and in a strange environment probably toughened him up mentally and he was a slightly different horse when he came back.

"His condition was nowhere near where I believed it should have been when he first came home but he whacked the weight on quickly and he did well in the stable. I wanted to start him off in the Newmarket because it has been traditionally a good race for stayers who can sprint well fresh and I had the best front-running stayer in the state and I knew he was very capable of running very fast times over that distance early in his prep."

The Cleaner went into the 2013 Newmarket without a trial because Mick knew a trial would take the edge off him. Maskiell was booked for the ride a month in advance but that plan was thrown into disarray when the young Tasmanian rider produced another positive swab to a prohibited substance emanating after a swab sample taken at a meeting at Kyneton the day after the Melbourne Cup. The subsequent inquiry was to deliver the worse possible outcome for Maskiell who was disqualified for 18 months (later reduced to six months) and the only way back was to endure structured rehabilitation courses. Almost three years on Maskiell remains out of the game, still battling his demons, although his dream of returning to race riding could still eventuate if he remains vigilant in his pursuit to get clean.

With Maskiell out of the equation Mick turned to veteran Victorian rider Darren Gauci, a regular visitor to Tasmania during carnival time, and a jockey with a reputation as being a genius on front-runners. The Newmarket field was strong with the Leon Wells-trained mares, Rebel Bride and Black 'N' Tough, both in terrific form. Kelvin Bourke was upbeat about the chances of Bocuse who had come to the race with reasonable form on country tracks in Victoria. The connections of Geegees Blackflash were again spruiking a first-up victory for their stable champ and Barry Campbell's star three-year-old from the previous season, Arenzano, had been powering her way to solid wins in open company and was backed in to start the second elect at $4.10 with Rebel Bride the favourite at $2.80.

"I had a good feeling about the race because the horse was spot on and I thought that all Gauci needed to do was rate him well and he'd be a big show. My only concern was that with the two mares of Leon Wells (Black 'N' Tough and Rebel Bride) in the race there was probably going to be plenty of pressure up front but I was confident that if it got into a dogfight Bill would come out on top even though the 1200 metres was not his go."

The Cleaner began like a shot but Gauci had to bustle him to hold the rails and Rebel Bride, with Craig Newitt on top, rode shotgun at the leader's girth while Brendon McCoull settled Black 'N' Tough just off the speed three-wide without cover.

Rebel Bride surged to the front 300m out and was being hailed the winner but The Cleaner fought back and then McCoull got to work on Black 'N' Tough ($4.60) and she went on to defeat the fast-finishing Bocuse ($14.60) with The Cleaner ($16.40) just ahead of Geegees Blackflash and Rebel Bride dead-heating for fourth. Geegees Blackflash had dashed home after being held up at a crucial stage and while he was unplaced there were smiles all round in the Luttrell camp post-race. Mick was ecstatic after the race as were the owners. The trip interstate had done The Cleaner no harm and they could now move ahead with added confidence.

A month later Mick entered The Cleaner in the weight-for-age Kevin Sharkie Tasmanian Stakes over 1600 metres in Hobart, the same race that had given Maskiell his first Listed winner on The Cleaner a year prior. Gauci was flown in for the ride and punters rallied for the horse sending his price tumbling into $2.20.

But there was an air of confidence in the support for Geegees Blackflash, into $3.20 second favourite, and that push was even stronger close to race start time courtesy of a buzz around the track that maybe The Flash's stablemate, renowned front-runner Pengalas Gee Gee at $103, might take on The Cleaner, a ploy that might prove the undoing of the favourite.

Gauci urged The Cleaner from the gates but so too did apprentice rider Siggy Carr who bustled Pengalas Gee Gee to find the spot outside of the leader. The pair travelled at what looked to be breakneck speed while Black 'N' Tough settled third with Brendon McCoull giggling to himself at what was taking place 15 lengths in front of him at the halfway mark.

Gauci tried to ease The Cleaner and let Pengalas Gee Gee roll to the front but the horse had a full head of steam and wasn't about to back off. At the home turn The Cleaner finally shrugged off the pest on his outside but he had exhausted his energy supply and this left Geegees Blackflash and Black 'N' Tough to fight out the finish with the mare emerging the winner by a half-length with Geegees Blackflash running out of gas near the line.

It was the last race of the day and as the connections of Black 'N' Tough celebrated the win the mood back at The Cleaner's stall was black. The owners were waiting for the trainer and owners of Geegees Blackflash to return so that they could vent their disapproval at what they believed to be spiteful tactics.

The matter was dealt with by the stewards who opened an inquiry into the riding tactics on Pengalas Gee Gee, but after taking evidence from that horse's trainer John Luttrell, owner Paul Geard, rider Carr as well as Mick and Gauci, stewards found there was no charge to answer and closed the inquiry, although they issued Luttrell with a warning that he should, in future, ensure that his instructions would allow his riders more flexibility when circumstances alter during a race.

The inquiry took four weeks to conclude and in the meantime The Cleaner would line up in the Ray Trinder Quality Handicap over 1600 metres in Launceston on New Year's Eve and Pengalas Gee Gee was at it again, only this time it appeared a more blatant assault on The Cleaner. In a small field of six, The Cleaner, the $2.40 second favourite behind Geegees Blackflash ($1.90), strolled to the lead with his new rider Anthony Darmanin aboard while Pengalas Gee Gee missed the start and was last on settling. It looked as if everyone had learned their lesson from the Hobart experience but apprentice Rhonda Mangan, who was the horse's regular trackwork rider, had other ideas and sent the $33.60 chance Pengalas Gee Gee around the field to again sit outside of The Cleaner. She then proceeded to urge her charge forward firing up The Cleaner and forcing Darmanin to call on every ounce of strength to hold his horse back.

Pengalas Gee Gee dropped off quickly when they reached the home turn but this time Geegees Blackflash was poised to pounce and gathered in The Cleaner about 200 metres out and went on to win by over a length.

The tactics again forced stewards to take action and this time hefty penalties resulted with Mangan being ousted for five meetings. Owner Paul Geard copped a $10,000 fine and Luttrell was fined $3000.

All three appealed and each appeal was upheld by the Tasmanian Racing Appeals Board (TRAB) with the chairman Tim Cox concluding that in the view of the TRAB the evidence in each case fell short of establishing that the instructions given would have inevitably deprived Pengalas Gee Gee of a full opportunity to win or finish in the best possible position in the race.

Mick was appalled at the outcome of the appeal but he took it all in his stride and focused on where he would aim The Cleaner next. He picked out the Piping Lane Handicap over 2000 metres at Flemington, a race named in honour of Tasmania's last Melbourne Cup winner (1970). Piping Lane was owned by Ray Trinder and ridden in the Cup by a young John Letts.

The Cleaner at $14, led and finished second yet again. It seemed the horse had forgotten how to win. Maybe it was him being softened up in the two races in Tasmania that had the horse's mind frazzled or maybe he was just tired of doing all the hard work in his races. Mick was keen to have another shot at the Hobart Cup so he used the weight-for-age Jockey Club Cup over 2200 metres in Hobart on February 2 as the horse's lead-up to the big race to be run on February 14. There was no Pengalas Gee Gee in this assignment but again The Cleaner had to settle for second, to another Geard-owned galloper in Gee Gee's La Quita who finished over the top of The Cleaner after being backed from $11 to $7.80, while those who took the $1.30 about The Cleaner were last seen looking to borrow enough for the fare home.

Undeterred by the flop Mick proceeded with his original plan to tackle the Hobart Cup but again The Cleaner failed to run out a strong 2400 metres and while game he finished fifth of nine beaten more than six lengths. The race was won by Epingle, prepared at Cranbourne by top Victorian trainer Mick Kent and ridden by class act Craig Williams.

Epingle and Williams would go on to win the Launceston Cup to earn the owner and trainer an equal share of the $100,000 Cups Double Bonus that was offered to the connections of any horse who could win both major Tasmanian cups in the same season.

After The Cleaner failed in the Hobart Cup Mick finally convinced the owners that he was not a 2400-metre horse. Mick gave the 2400-metre Launceston Cup a miss and freshened him up for a crack at the Listed $100,000 George Adams Plate at weight-for-age over 1600 metres at Launceston on February 26. It's no easy task for a horse to drop back in distance after enduring a stayer's preparation. The horse was also close to the end of his tether, a point that also weighed heavily on Mick's mind in the days leading up to the race.

"I had about two weeks to freshen him up. He loved the mile in Launceston and I was confident he could win because there was nothing else likely to run in the race that could challenge him in front, so I thought that as long as he was well in himself we'd run him. I'm bloody glad I did because he was magnificent."

With Darmanin retaining the ride The Cleaner delivered an awesome display in the best performance of the preparation. He toyed with his rivals as he made every post a winner on his way to a two-length win over Jakcorijim. Mick had achieved his best training feat. The owners had had a decent bet with as much as $5 offered before he firmed late to start at $4.60. The $2.20 favourite Road Trippin', from Victoria, was under pressure turning for home and battled into fifth spot but almost six lengths from the winner.

When Mick got home that night he put The Cleaner in his paddock at the back of the stables, happy and content that the horse had done well despite having only won one of his seven starts through the preparation but it was also while watching the horse stroll around his yard that he began thinking about the possibility of aiming him at the richest and most prestigious weight-for-age race in Australasia—the G1 Cox Plate at Moonee Valley.

20

Shooting for the Stars

THE Cleaner had yet to make a real impact on the mainland, at least at the top level. Most of the pundits were aware of him but none rated him a horse capable of getting a start in a Cox Plate, let alone winning one. But it was the race Mick had set his sights on at the end of his 2013-14 campaign.

He mentioned the idea to the owners but to nobody else for fear they would think he'd finally lost it. Mick had never been backward in blurting out what was on his mind but this audacious plan had to be carefully crafted. Should he declare his hand he would no doubt cop all sorts of negative feedback so this time he would keep his cards close to his chest. He had studied the lead-up races to the Cox Plate and the one he'd settled on was the Dato Tan Chin Nam Stakes, formerly known as the Feehan Stakes, to be run over 1600 metres at Moonee Valley in early September. Mick liked this race because the winner gained a ballot-free entry into the Cox Plate. If he was right it would be The Cleaner's—and his—ticket to stardom.

The Cleaner was back in work 10 days after winning the George Adams

Plate but that was nothing new to the horse who seemed to prefer being in work than spelling in a paddock. His trial on his home track three weeks before venturing to Melbourne to kick off his Cox Plate program was modest, to say the least.

Young Longford apprentice Sherry Barr was on top and she thought it was Christmas guiding the local hero around over 700 metres on May 6. The trial was won by Bon Benito, a lightly raced Bon Hoffa filly with The Cleaner back third. Soon after, The Cleaner was back on the boat to Melbourne to line up in a heat of the Winter Championship at Flemington on May 24. Anthony Darmanin retained the ride and while he had to settle for second there was only a head between him and the winner, Limes, a John O'Shea-trained gelding with excellent form in Melbourne and Sydney.

A month later The Cleaner was back for round two of his path to the Cox Plate and after a night relaxing at Pine Lodge he was off to Moonee Valley to line up in the Travis Harrison Cup over 1600 metres. Punters warmed to The Cleaner and sent him around the $3.20 favourite. This time Darmanin rated his charge perfectly and when he was asked to extend, The Cleaner forged clear and went on to win by three lengths. The media swarmed around Mick as Darmanin brought The Cleaner back to the enclosure. Mick was tempted to reveal his long-range plan, but bit his tongue and fended off any questions about where he might be headed with the horse. One scribe asked that very question and as quick as a flash Mick replied: "He's heading back home to Tassie. We leave tonight." There was an air of authority about this latest win and Mick knew it.

"You can always tell when a horse is on top of his game and what I saw in him before and after that race was enough to tell me I might be on the right track about the Cox Plate."

His next mission was the Listed Winter Championship Final carrying prizemoney of $152,000 ($90,000 to the winner) and Mick and the owners were confident they would be spending the lion's share of it. The

Cleaner and his trainer arrived safely the day before the race, with the Bass Strait crossing one of the smoothest in weeks. Mick whacked a lead rope on the horse and led him to the training track at Pine Lodge. He then disengaged the clip from the horse's headstall and The Cleaner just followed his trainer around for two laps and then they headed back to a holding yard that had been readied for him by Pine Lodge's owner Bill Le Sueur.

"Pine Lodge was the perfect place for us to stay because the accommodation was great for both me and the horse. They treated the horse like one of their own and he was just as at home there as he was back at my stables."

The Cleaner faced a slow track at Flemington but he had proven he could handle all types of going, although heavy tracks had a tendency to slow him down a little. He drew wide in gate 12 but there was a decent run to the first turn so that wasn't going to present any problem. As usual The Cleaner was allowed to bowl along at his leisure with the other riders aware that taking him on would be at their own peril. He was cruising in the lead and at the 800-metre peg Darmanin allowed him a bit more rein and the tempo increased with the rider confident that the new speed he put into the race would have a few of his main rivals off the bit and chasing hard.

Back in the field Michelle Payne had Ciaron Maher's four-year-old Akavoroun travelling sweetly, without having spent much energy she called on him to set out after the leader. He made ground quickly but still spotted The Cleaner about 10 lengths as they approached the home turn. Four hundred metres out Payne switched course and aimed her charge toward the outside of the track and once in the fast lane Akavoroun ($6) rushed home and hit the line almost a length clear of The Cleaner ($9) who battled gamely to the line. For the first time in three preparations Mick was upset over the ride.

"When Darmanin got off I told him in no uncertain terms what I thought of the ride. He reckoned my horse had had enough so he stopped riding him hard. I thought that was the most ridiculous thing I'd ever heard because every time he'd ridden the horse he knew how much he responded to strong riding. In the end I accepted what he said and moved on, but I think he knew that was going to be the last time he sat on The Cleaner. If I was going to put the horse in Group races further down the track I needed to know that the rider was going to be serious on the horse from start to finish."

Darmanin had been dumped over one ride but in the racing game trainers and jockeys are constantly making moves that neither party, at times, can fathom.

"I was very disappointed when I was sacked from The Cleaner," Darmanin said, "but in this game you can be only as good as your last ride and even though I didn't think I did too much wrong I had to take it on the chin and move on. I loved riding The Cleaner. He was such a good ride because once he got to the front he always relaxed. You had to get up him to keep him going but he was just so tough.

"I still think his best distance was 1600 metres and while he could get 2000 metres, he was more vulnerable near the end of those races. To win the races that he did was a credit to both the horse and the trainer. I always got on well with Mick and I still get on well with him. What happened with me and him was just business. I would have no hesitation in getting on one of Mick's horses. He's a very good trainer and you don't get the results that he did with The Cleaner without being good."

THERE was a race at Moonee Valley in early August that looked tempting so Mick nominated The Cleaner for the 1600-metre open handicap. He chased Noel Callow to ride. He was rapt when the 'The Enforcer' accepted the offer. Callow earned the nickname during a two-year stint in Singapore and Malaysia courtesy of his strong riding technique and it was a nickname that he wore as a badge of honour in Singapore where hard whip riding is encouraged. Australia had just introduced strict rules on whip use so if Callow was to deliver what

Mick Burles knew he had a good horse in his midst long before The Cleaner raced. Here he looks up and gives his stable star an admiring look after a trackwork gallop.
(PHOTO: PETER STAPLES)

The Cleaner spent most of his leisure time in his paddock behind his Longford stables. It was his home away from the racetrack. (PHOTO: PETER STAPLES)

Jason Maskiell riding The Cleaner to win a quality handicap in Launceston in January 2013. (PHOTO: PETER STAPLES)

Mick was a big supporter of Jason Maskiell and nobody was as disappointed as Mick when the whiz kid jockey from Longford fell victim to illicit drugs. (PHOTO: PETER STAPLES)

Magic Millions used the success of The Cleaner to help promote its 2015 Tasmanian Yearling Sale. This is the banner that created a lot of attention. A half-brother to The Cleaner topped the sale at $100,000. (PHOTO: PETER STAPLES)

One of The Cleaner's owners, Bill Fawdry, attended the 2016 Tasmanian Magic Millions Yearling sale with the hope of finding another The Cleaner. Here he is with his daughter Lisa as they work their way through the sale catalogue. (PHOTO: PETER STAPLES)

The Cleaner with one of his trackwork riders David Quinn. It would be Quinn who played a role in the rift between Mick and the horse's owners that eventually led to the horse being taken from Mick. (PHOTO: PETER STAPLES)

Karl Rhodes was The Cleaner's trackwork rider for his first attempt at the Cox Plate (2014). Rhodes eventually branched out as a trainer in his own right but sadly was disqualified over a positive swab to one of his horses.

Mick's stable foreman Mikayla Flack. She saw first-hand how The Cleaner and Mick developed a special bond. Here she tends to "Bill" after a track gallop. (PHOTOS: PETER STAPLES)

Anthony Darmanin was one of a handful of jockeys who played a role in The Cleaner's rise to the top. Here he is partnering The Cleaner to victory in the $100,000 weight-for-age George Adams Plate in Launceston in 2014. (PHOTO: PETER STAPLES)

Mick was keen to get Noel Callow on The Cleaner as he believed that of all the jockeys who were available he would best suit the horse because of his aggressive riding style. Here Callow brings The Cleaner back to the unsaddling enclosure after finishing third in the Group 1 Underwood Stakes in 2015. (PHOTO: SHARON CHAPMAN)

Steven Arnold won aboard The Cleaner at his first two rides. Here he is about to give the gelding a well-deserved pat after winning the Dato' Tan Chin Nam Stakes at Moonee Valley in 2014.
(PHOTO: SHARON CHAPMAN)

The Cleaner's owners and travelling entourage celebrate another win: (L-R) owner Paul Burt, Mick, Melbourne strapper Glen Burton, owner Bill Fawdry, friend of Burt's Harry Butler, owner Jim Lowish and Tasmanian horse transporter Vern Poke. (PHOTO: SHARON CHAPMAN)

Children from two schools in Longford gathered to give The Cleaner a big send-off for his first attempt at the Cox Plate in 2014. (PHOTO: PETER STAPLES)

Mick proudly displays the sale docket for a filly by Anacheeva that he purchased for $27,000 at the 2016 Tasmanian Magic Millions Yearling Sale.

(PHOTO: PETER STAPLES)

Mick required he would have to do it within the guidelines set down by Australian stewards.

Mick was taken ill and was unable to travel to Melbourne. He had no option but to despatch his stablehand David Quinn to act as travelling foreman. Mick had copped a bad bout of the flu and despite pumping himself full of drugs in the week leading up to the race he was unable to fend off the virus.

"I knew if I travelled to Melbourne with the flu I'd end up in hospital so I called the owners and told them what was happening and I sent Quinny to look after the horse. I was happy enough to have him take care of Bill because he had been riding him in trackwork and had got on well with the horse."

It was August 2, and Victoria's first metropolitan meeting of the new racing season with The Cleaner having celebrated his sixth birthday the day before. Callow was pumped about being the horse's new partner and the owners were cashed up and ready to do battle with the bookies, despite The Cleaner having to carry topweight of 60.5 kg. There were no luxury odds on offer with $2.70 the best bet. He firmed to start the $2.30 favourite while Darren Gauci's mount Tristram's Sun, from the Robbie Laing yard, had eased slightly to be the second elect at $5.

What Callow didn't count on was Ken Keys' gelding First Course, with Steve Baster on top, taking him on and they engaged in a battle to the home turn. Mick thought it was Pengalas Gee Gee revisited, but Callow never panicked, he just kept urging on his mount. To the rider's surprise The Cleaner edged clear despite the big weight and on the line he had a length and a quarter to spare. Callow couldn't believe the courage shown by the horse. When he dismounted he just shook his head, looked at the owners and said: "How the hell did he win?" Hanging on every word, the reporters were all of a sudden interested in this horse from Tasmania. The whispers about him being the next Vo Rogue and Mick being compared to that horse's trainer, the late Vic Rail, were now gaining momentum.

It was a herculean effort under such a weight but Mick knew the opposition was a far cry from what he'd be taking on when he stepped up to Group level. Mick was counting on Callow sticking with the horse for the rest of his campaign but the rider dropped a bombshell when he called Mick to tell him he had accepted an offer to ride overseas and he wouldn't be able to ride his horse for the balance of his campaign.

"I had to find a rider and fast because the horse's next start was in the Dato Tan Chin Nam Stakes on September 6, and I had two weeks to find a suitable jockey. My first choice was Steve Arnold and bugger me if he didn't accept the ride as soon as I spoke to him. I couldn't believe my luck. Steve is a brilliant rider. I thought that if he was good enough for Bart Cummings then he'd be good enough for me." Arnold had ridden Cummings' champion So You Think to win the 2010 Cox Plate.

BY now Mick had revealed his Cox Plate plans to all and sundry and even though most in the game thought he was chasing rainbows the horse was making a statement by hitting a home run every time he stepped up to the plate. The media was now infatuated with The Cleaner and loved the story behind his knockabout trainer. The Cleaner was now dubbed the 'Longford Lion' and horse and trainer were now one win away from realising Mick's crazy dream. Win the $251,500 Dato ($151,500 to the winner), and he was in the Cox Plate. The lead-up to the race was electric and the Moonee Valley Racing Club was on board promoting the race on the back of The Cleaner story. Could a horse that cost a modest $10,000 at a Tasmanian yearling sale and be trained from a sleepy hollow in the middle of the smallest state in Australia wander its way into one of the richest and most prestigious weight-for-age races in the world?

Mick felt the pressure creep into the stable the week leading up to the race. Longford was abuzz with the thought of the town boasting a Cox Plate runner. Mick tried to keep a lid on it but to no avail; the local media was hot for the story. He was going through his usual pack of 30 cigs a day but the added pressure was starting to take its toll on his emphysema.

"At one stage I felt like telling everyone to just leave me alone but

I knew they were all just excited about the horse having a chance of getting into a Cox Plate. It's funny how one day you're just an old knockabout trainer with a crazy pipedream and the next you're the flavour of the month and every bastard wants to know you."

Mick and his stable star again travelled to Melbourne on the Spirit of Tasmania only this time the vessel tackled a seven-metre swell. So turbulent was the crossing Mick was tossed out of his bunk as he slept. But when The Cleaner stepped off the truck at Pine Lodge there wasn't a hair out of place, although the same couldn't be said for Mick.

After a quiet relaxing night at their Oaklands Junction lodgings it was off to the Valley for what would be The Cleaner's biggest test. Mick kept thinking about that saying, 'one day a rooster, a feather duster the next', and he wondered which one that he and the horse would be at the end of the race.

THE atmosphere was charged as The Cleaner strolled into the parade ring at the back of the main grandstand. Mick was starting to warm to all the attention; he was even propositioned as he was about to wander off to retrieve the saddle from the jockeys' room.

"I couldn't believe it when this nice lookin' sheila comes up and asks if I'd like to stay at her place for the night. You could have knocked me over with a feather. Of course I thanked her kindly for the offer but would have to refuse as I was going back home that night. But I did tell her she was welcome to stay with me if she ever got to Tassie!"

Mick was surprisingly calm as he manoeuvred his way through the crowd to secure a spot to watch the race. He glanced over at the owners who stood to his right and said, "This is it boys. It'll be the big time or the back yard—good luck." Punters all over Australia had backed The Cleaner to start the $4.40 favourite in his first try at Group 2 level.

Arnold urged The Cleaner from the gates and from barrier two he had no trouble rolling straight to the front. He set a good tempo to the 600m where Arnold upped the pace to try and set the opposition too great a task. The Cleaner had covered the first 1000 metres in a tick under a minute, and hit a flat spot 500 metres out but he quickly regained his momentum and then fought hard all the way home to hit the line almost a length clear of Mourinho ($14), with Craig Newitt aboard, while Chris Waller's Cups hope, the import Foreteller ($7) rattled home from near last to grab third.

When Newitt dismounted from Mourinho he leaned over the winner's stall, gave Mick a wink and said, "Well done Mick but give a break mate. I'm sick to death of looking at your horse's arse."

It was pandemonium at the winner's stall with every journalist wanting to get first grab with Mick. The old codger was in tears when the on-course TV presenter reached him and the cameras captured, for the first time, what the horse really meant to Mick. Back home in the clubs, pubs and hotels and everywhere else that showed the race, Tasmanian fans were screaming at the monitor, urging their new hero over the line. It was the same all over Australia. The Cleaner had arrived as a genuine Group horse and Mick's pipedream was about to be realised.

"To be honest I felt as if we'd already won the Cox Plate. I was so excited I have no recollection of what I said to the media but I knew that we were going to the Cox Plate and nobody could stop us. It was one of the best feelings I've ever had in my life. Better than sex and that's sayin' somethin'."

In Tasmania the TV stations were on the phone to Mick to find out when the horse would be home and when Mick would be available for an interview. The charismatic trainer and his bold frontrunner had struck a nerve with the public, as evidenced by the social media frenzy post race with comments and best wishes for both horse and trainer coming from all corners of the nation. Many tweets and Facebook entries were accompanied by a video of the race that went viral.

ONCE the buzz had faded, Mick focused on selecting which race would be the horse's final lead-up to the Cox Plate. He narrowed it down to either the G1 Underwood Stakes at weight-for-age over 1800 metres at Caulfield or to return to The Valley and tackle the $201,500 G3 JRA Cup over the Cox Plate distance of 2040 metres to be run four weeks before the big one. He chose the latter.

There were still a couple of hurdles to jump before the Cox Plate but realistically all Mick had to do was keep the horse injury-free and The Cleaner would be rubbing shoulders with some of the best weight-for-age gallopers in the world. The preparation for the JRA Cup went smoothly and again there were no problems with the trip across. The JRA Cup boasted some of the early favourites for the Caulfield and Melbourne Cups including Sangster, Precedence, Big Memory and Mr O'Ceirin, while Mourinho was again expected to make his presence felt as he sought a berth in the Cox Plate.

It was to be a big test and from gate nine in the field of 12 the horse would need to be ridden with a bit more patience than normal. There was a lot of genuine early speed inside him. Arnold stuck to the game plan and gradually worked his way across the field and crossed to the front shortly after passing the winning post the first time.

With a lapful of horse under him Arnold asked The Cleaner to increase the tempo 800 metres out and he obliged, pinching a three-length break on his rivals at the 500-metre mark but he looked vulnerable when Sangster, who had enjoyed a cushy run on the rails, emerged to make his move. But The Cleaner refused to wilt and he had enough in reserve to defeat the 2011 VRC Derby winner, Sangster, by a head with Mourinho a close-up third. Arnold was two from two on The Cleaner and as he was removing the saddle he told Mick that he only had to keep the horse in that form and he'd give the Cox Plate a real shake.

"I told Steve that if he could get a better ride in the Cox Plate then he should take it but he just shook his head and said: "I won't get a better ride than this."

21

On Media Street

IN the weeks leading up to the 2014 Cox Plate Mick was slowed by his respiratory condition but he refused to let anything interfere with The Cleaner's training. He had somehow managed to get his best mate into a Cox Plate and he wasn't about to miss out on what could be the greatest moment of his training life.

Bill Fawdry was concerned about the state of Mick's health, so on the suggestion of well-known Channel Seven TV reporter, the former Longford lad, Neil Kearney, he popped over to the stables and confiscated Mick's phone and told him he'd vet the calls so he might have some peace for a few days.

Mick was about to venture where no other Tasmanian trainer had travelled. Tasmanian-bred and owned gelding Sydeston had been to multiple Cox Plates and was placed in two and Alfa had earned a berth in one but both were trained on the mainland by the late Bob Hoysted and Bart Cummings respectively.

"Being the first Tassie trainer to have a runner in a Cox Plate made me feel pretty good. When I was a kid a teacher once told me I'd never amount to anything. He's dead now but if he wasn't I'd probably seek him out and give him a gander at a few newspaper clippings."

The Cleaner was taking all of the fuss in his stride. Every time Mick gave the horse a gallop at the Longford track there was at least one TV crew capturing the horse's every move. And Mick's too.

Longford was virtually unknown until The Cleaner came along. The township had ben founded in 1814 by Newman Williatt, the first postmaster in Launceston. Renowned for its fertile soil and roaming plains the area was first identified as an ideal region for the settlement of farmers and stock breeders. But it also is famous as having been a haven for bushrangers.

Mick 's eyes lit up when he was told of the town's connection to bushrangers at a special function put on by the Longford Shire Council to congratulate Mick and his horse for grabbing a berth in the Cox Plate. "I reckon if I'd have lived in the early 1800s I'd have probably been a bushranger," he said with a broad smile on his dial.

If Mick needed any convincing that he should take better care of himself, it came two weeks out from the Cox Plate when he had to be admitted to hospital. He had trouble breathing and at one point had passed out in his easy chair and woke to find his fingers toes and lips had turned blue. He immediately carted himself off to hospital where he stayed for three days.

"I had my pipes cleaned out and I felt a whole lot better," he said. "I've only got one lung and sometimes that only operates at half strength so if I get a cold or worse, the flu, it knocks me totally. I can't get the muck off my chest and it causes all sorts of problems. I was told that I might get a lung transplant if I gave up the smokes and I've been trying to do that for ages."

Fawdry was with Mick when he was visited in hospital by his specialist and what the doctors told Mick that day convinced Fawdry his trainer was in more than a bit of trouble.

"These two doctors walked into Mick's room and I was sitting in the chair bedside his bed when one of them said he was confident he could perform a surgery and prescribe medication that would help fix Mick's problem but then he added that because he was still a smoker he might not qualify for the procedure.

"It made me think that maybe Mick was in worse shape than I first thought," Fawdry said.

Mick felt much better when he strolled out of the Launceston General Hospital but what the doctor had told Mick in front of Fawdry a day earlier worried the part-owner, and would stay in his mind for many months.

Having The Cleaner at his top for the biggest race of his life was all Mick could think about. He had many a sleepless night and with the media continually pestering him for a grab had him reaching for his inhaler more often than usual, but it was the repetitive questions that wound Mick up.

"I started to think these journalists were reading from a script. The questions were the same and I just got sick of it, although I played a bit of a game with one fella who rang me from one of the racing websites. I gave him a couple of weird answers just to see if he'd print them and he did. Who knows what some of the others wrote. All this media stuff was still new to me but I did the best I could."

MICK had kept The Cleaner to the same training routine as he had for the JRA Cup but he needed to make sure the horse didn't leave anything of value on the training track in the week leading up to the big race. The Cleaner knew every blade of grass on the Longford track and on the Tuesday morning before the Cox Plate, Mick had his stable foreman Mikayla Flack throw the saddle on the stable star for what would be his final gallop before the race. Mick made his way down to the tiny grandstand where he sat with stopwatch in hand. The grandstand had been burned down a decade beforehand and rebuilt, thanks to the devotion of the late Jim Osborne after whom the stand is now named.

Mick waited for trackwork rider Karl Rhodes to give the horse a squeeze at the 600m before he readied the timing device and when The Cleaner crossed the 400m mark Mick hit the go button on the stopwatch and when he clicked it again at the winning post he looked down and liked what he saw. The Cleaner had run his last 400m in 21.7 seconds. Another local trainer, John Blacker, who also clocked him, remarked that he had never seen a better sectional at the track in all his years at Longford.

"It was a super gallop and I said then that if he couldn't win a Cox Plate on that gallop then he'd never win one," said Blacker.

It was a winning track gallop and Mick was sure that all the horse needed to have a fighting chance in the race was a decent barrier. At the official barrier draw later that day, the quiet one of the three owners, Jim Lowish, who had been elected to make the trip to Melbourne to attend the function, sat nervously waiting for The Cleaner's name to be read out by chief steward Terry Bailey. The general consensus was that barrier one was definitely not on the wish list and the same applied to barriers 2 and 13.

By the time The Cleaner's name was pulled from the barrel there were only a handful of numbers remaining and Lowish plucked barrier 14—the outside gate. Steve Arnold would just have to be at the top of his game to help his mount overcome what looked to be the worst possible gate for a likely race leader.

WHEN Vern Poke's truck chugged in to Mick's stables to pick up The Cleaner on the Thursday afternoon before the Cox Plate it was greeted by a media frenzy. The local council had arranged to have representatives there for the horse's departure and school children from both schools in the area lined the streets to form a guard of honour as the truck rolled down Anstey Street en route to Devonport.

Mick had spent a half an hour signing autographs and he interrupted the loading of the horse to allow some of the kids to have photographs taken with horse and trainer. The children lapped it up and so did The Cleaner. It's always advisable to be wary when near a finely-tuned racehorse but this fellow was unique. The kids were brushing up against his legs when trying to take up positions for the photos but he just stood there unflustered. If he had been any more relaxed he would have been comatose.

"It was bloody unbelievable. I felt like a movie star and the horse was loving it too. I even shed a tear or two because I was rapt that so many people had gone to the trouble of being there to wish us well. The drive to Devonport was pretty good after that send off but once we reached the boat everything was back to normal, although one TV crew was there to greet us but there was not much we could do for them. I wasn't about to unload the horse while we were waiting in the queue to get on the boat."

The overnight journey across the strait was pleasant enough but Mick spent most of the night walking the decks, unable to sleep. Not allowed to go below to check on his steed, he eventually made his way to his room and bunked down for what ended up being not quite two hours of restless slumber. As soon as he and Vern were allowed below to check on the horse Mick made a beeline to the truck to see how he'd travelled. He need not have worried. The horse was chomping on some hay and was ready for the trip to Pine Lodge.

Mick was hoping for a lean day with the media but no sooner had the truck rolled off the Spirit of Tasmania he was greeted by a bevy of TV crews and photographers all clambering around the truck trying to get that special shot that might find its way onto the front or back pages of Saturday's papers or that evening's TV sports reports.

When the truck pulled into Pine Lodge it was another media fest. Camera crews lined the driveway, scribes were checking their tape recorders and TV presenters were having the last touches of make-up applied. It was a circus with Mick and The Cleaner the star attractions. Mick had been shocked by the amount of interest the Tasmanian media had shown in him and the horse but he was absolutely gobsmacked when he landed in Melbourne.

With the interviews at Pine Lodge done and dusted Mick grabbed a lead rope and took The Cleaner up to the training track for the mandatory two-lap walk and then the horse was put into his paddock and left to his own devices until late that afternoon.

22

Race Day

CHANNEL Seven's broadcast of the race meeting on free-to-air TV included a direct cross to Longford where Neil Kearney had set up camp in the middle of town. Every so often viewers all over Australia would get a sneak peek at the home of The Cleaner. Longford was suddenly famous!

The trip to Moonee Valley was uneventful and when Mick led The Cleaner into his stall the horse eased his rear end to one side and started gnawing on his lead rope, customary practice for the horse at the races. Mick, dressed in his black suit, black shirt and sky blue tie matching his racing colours, leaned up against the side of the stripping stall nodding to anyone who was showing an interest in his ordinary looking bay gelding. A Melbourne-based strapper was assigned to The Cleaner but Mick was starting to grow weary of his inability to follow instructions.

"The strapper kept pissing off with the horse taking him for walks so I told him not to. I went for a leak and when I returned the horse was gone again. I got fairly shitty with him and told him that if he continued to do that he could piss off. He said that everyone else liked their horses walked regularly while they waited for their race. I told him I didn't because it made them fidgety and anxious. If Bill's left alone all he'll do is chew on his lead rope and that relaxes him. He finally agreed not to do it again."

Steve Arnold spent a few minutes limbering up as the owners and Mick awaited the jockey's arrival in the mounting yard. When he strolled out of the jockeys' room he cast a shadow over most of his counterparts. Arnold is tall for a jockey, and his weight restricts his riding opportunities. There were no instructions required from Mick. He knew Arnold had done his homework, and had learned the horse's racing pattern from the JRA Cup win. The whole world knew he was on the likely leader. There was little for Mick to say to his jockey other than 'good luck and bring home the bacon'.

Mick was in another world as the field marched their way on to the track to do their preliminary workouts on the way to the barrier. Mick had done everything in his power to have his horse ready for his toughest assignment. As he stood in the enclosure, behind where the jockeys return to scale after the race, he wondered what life might be like should The Cleaner be able to fend off some of the best middle distance gallopers in the world.

"As I was getting into position to watch the race I had all these memories flashing through my mind. I thought of my first winner as a trainer, Irish Reaction, then where I was when I was a kid riding my horse Tom and how blessed I was to be mixing it with the likes of Chris Waller, Gai Waterhouse and John O'Shea. It probably didn't mater whether Bill won or lost. I would always be the first Tasmanian trainer to have a runner in a Cox Plate. Gee, I felt good."

The race, carrying prizemoney of $3 million, with prizemoney down to eighth ($100,000) unfolded as expected with The Cleaner forced to do a lot of bustling work to find the front. He was five-wide as the field past the winning post the first time with Gai Waterhouse's three-year-old pair, Wandjina, a lightweight with 49.5 kg, able to land on the rails with his stablemate Almalad caught three-wide outside of Side Glance; that trio kept the Tasmanian stuck on a limb.

It wasn't until the field had travelled 800 metres that Arnold was able to finally secure the lead. When he called on his mount to extend 600 metres from home he was game as ever, as he laid his ears back and stretched his legs as far as they would extend. By the time he reached the home turn there were challengers galore, with the exception of Waterhouse's three-year-olds that had taken on a bit more than they could chew and were falling away. The gallant grey Fawkner loomed to win and racecaller Greg Miles had his eye on Adelaide who had spent no juice early settling last but was making ground quickly, under hard riding by superstar jockey Ryan Moore.

Adelaide was the widest runner at the top of the short home straight, but was able to power home in a blanket finish to score by neck from Lloyd Williams' Fawkner (Nick Hall) with Nash Rawiller's mount Silent Achiever a half-head away third.

The Cleaner was game in defeat finishing ninth and in between the three-year-olds Sweynesse, from the John O'Shea stable, and Wandjina. Waterhouse's other runner, Almalad was more than 25 lengths away.

The work that The Cleaner had to do early had taken its toll. It was, after all, a Cox Plate and no horse could have expected to expend so much energy early and have enough in the tank to win the race, or even compete as well as did The Cleaner. To his credit The Cleaner, sent to the barriers a $15 chance, finished only 3.35 lengths from the winner in his first shot at Group 1 glory in the toughest WFA race in the land. Behind him were three Group 1 winners, Wandjina (who would take the 2015 Australian Guineas the following autumn), Sacred Falls (2012 NZ Guineas, 2013/14 Doncaster, 2014 George Main), and Royal Descent (2013 ATC Oaks). The tempo set by The Cleaner was responsible for one of the fastest run Cox Plates (2.03.76) since Might And Power covered the 2040 metres in 2m.03.54s in 1998.

The win of Adelaide, a three-year-old in the southern hemisphere, and previously a winner in Ireland and America, had confirmed the Cox Plate as a truly international event.

Mick was hoping Bill might manage to sneak into eighth spot to snare the $100,000 in prizemoney and at least cover the cost of accepting for the race and toss in some spare change. But it was never about the money for Mick. His best mate had given his all in what was his first try against the best and he almost got there.

Had it not been for the barrier and the energy it took to get to the front, it may have been a different story. Mick had a crack at the tactics used against his horse in post-race interviews and he claimed that probably none of them would ever win another race. He was right about one of them, Sweynesse, although he did finish a brave second to Hollowed Crown in the G1 Randwick Guineas the following March. Almalad was sold to Hong Kong after the Cox Plate and renamed Friends Of Ka Ying and could only manage a win in a restricted class two race at Sha Tin. However Wandjina, who had finished half a length behind The Cleaner did go on to win the Group 1 Australian Guineas at Flemington in the autumn.

MICK still believed The Cleaner had a Group 1 win in him so he looked towards the Emirates Stakes over 1600m on the last day of the VRC Spring Carnival a fortnight later. His horse had pulled up brilliantly from his Cox Plate outing and while there were some up and coming milers who had targeted the Flemington race Mick saw it as an opportunity for The Cleaner to finally get what he deserved—a Group 1 win.

When The Cleaner arrived home in Tasmania the media was still keen for an update and when Mick revealed he would be heading back to Melbourne for one last shot at a Group 1 some observers questioned the decision, with one reporter asking when Mick might give the horse a break. When Mick explained that the horse had come through the Cox Plate run way better than he expected, the journalist persisted with his line of questioning. In the end Mick just turned to him and said: "Mate. Leave the training and welfare of the horse to me and you just concentrate of learning how to write stories."

Mick was always better at media conferences when he was comfortable with the interviewer and it was never more evident when dealing with the veteran broadcaster and journalist Bruce 'Snowy' Clark.

Clark was MC at a press conference at Crown Casino on the eve of the 2014 Emirates Stakes, and he asked Mick what it was like for him having The Cleaner running in a race that had included a horse trained by the great Aidan O'Brien, Mick replied: "Aidan who?!"

"I don't mind doing interviews if I'm comfortable with the person with the microphone and I guess that's what makes Bruce such a top interviewer," Mick said.

The Cleaner, again with Arnold in the saddle, was sent out at good odds of $16 in the Emirates from a good gate (6). Again he would take the lead, and again he would lead well into the straight. This time, he was run down by the South Australian Hucklebuck, and the Darren Weir-trained Lucky Hussler. It was another game effort with the horse again lauded for his courageous fighting spirit, finishing just over a length from the winner. With the Melbourne Carnival all but over, Mick was left to ponder the horse's immediate future.

"I knew the horse had a Group 1 win in him and that the Emirates Stakes was his for the taking but the race just didn't quite play out as we expected."

Mick was keen to give The Cleaner a spell but with pressure coming from the owners to head to Western Australia in search of the elusive Group 1 the trainer surrendered and the horse was aimed at The Railway Stakes at Ascot on November 22, a fortnight after the Emirates. The long and exhausting trip to Perth would prove too much for both horse and trainer.

"I never wanted to go to Perth because everyone I'd spoken to who had made the trip said it had the potential to bugger the horse. It wasn't so much the flight to Perth but it was the effort getting onto the plane and then having to deal with the climate when we got there.

"It never went well. We spent six hours on the tarmac waiting to get loaded onto the plane and more delays in taking off and it took a fair bit out of him. He crashed his head through the roof of the truck while we were waiting to get him on the plane and while he didn't injure himself he was really stirred up and he was in a lather of sweat by the time he got on the plane. Then it was ages before we took off and both the horse and I were nervous wrecks by the time we got to Perth."

When they arrived in the west, there was a strong media contingent to greet the 'Longford Lion' who was now carrying the can for not just the Tasmanian racing industry but the entire state. There's no doubt star Tasmanian-owned and bred pacer Beautide helped lift the island state's harness racing profile with his back-to-back Inter Dominion successes (2014/15) ranking him one of the all-time best of his code. But what The Cleaner and Mick were doing was gold, promoting Tasmania as a great racing State.

MICK and The Cleaner were now a double act with the horse taking care of business on the track while Mick dealt with the media. "I have sort of learned how to answer a question without giving the whole game away but it took me a while to get the hang of it."

Some reporters were labelling the Railway Stakes as The Cleaner's big chance to win a Group 1 but after a few days settling in at Fred Kersley's stables on course at Ascot, Mick was starting to realise that he probably should have been more firm with the owners and stayed at home.

"I gave the horse a strong gallop on the Tuesday before the race and there were a few high profile trainers watching the gallop who said there was no horse that worked better on the track that day so that lifted my spirits a bit but something Fred Kersley told me brought me back to earth.

"Fred said my horse couldn't win the Railway Stakes with the weight he'd been allocated (58kg) and he added his former top horse Northerly wouldn't have been able win the race with that weight either so that sat me back on me arse—quick and smart." Northerly had won the 2000 Railway with just 51 kilos, and then took the east by storm, winning the Cox Plate twice, the Caulfield Cup, and The Australian Cup twice, among many other Group 1 races.

The build up to the Railway Stakes went as expected with most of the pundits predicting The Cleaner would lead but the smarties were adamant the Tassie champ would puncture when the pressure was applied at the business end.

The Cleaner, sent out a $5.50 favourite, showed his customary early speed to take control of the race but when rider Steve Arnold called on him to extend at the 600-metre peg the spring was uncoiled and he was unable to put a margin on them.

While The Cleaner kept whacking away trying as hard as he could to fight off the army of challengers the lightly weighted Elite Belle, the second favourite at $6, stormed to the lead 100 metres from home and went on to win by almost a length with Mick's stable star finishing ninth, three lengths from the winner. The words of Fred Kersley were still ringing loud in Mick's ears as eight runners swept past his champion over the concluding stages.

When Mick and The Cleaner returned home from Perth there was no fanfare this time, just an eerie silence as Vern Poke's truck rolled off the Spirit of Tasmania bound for home.

"When we finally arrived at the stables I think both me and the horse heaved a big sigh of relief because it had been a bastard of a trip and I was more worried about whether I'd have a horse to work with the following spring. But I just kept reminding myself that he is a tough bastard."

23

Back to Work

MICK gave his charge some time off and just under three months later The Cleaner, with his new trackwork rider David Quinn, was in an open trial at Longford finishing an eye-catching second to Huss Style over 700 metres. For The Cleaner's two previous preparations he had been ridden in trackwork by former Victorian horseman Karl Rhodes, regarded by Mick as the best trackwork rider he has had.

"Karl was a ripper rider who would do exactly as he was told and when you have that sort of a rider working with your good horse it takes a lot of the pressure off. He has great hands and he is one of those blokes who has a clock in his head and that's so important, especially with fast work."

But Rhodes had plans to take out a trainer's licence and establish a business of his own so he moved on—with Mick's blessing. Into the breach stepped Quinn who Mick was sure would fill the void. Rhodes achieved his goal and had his first winner as a trainer in Hobart not long after his licence was approved but about six months later he hit the headlines for all the wrong reasons. Rhodes' horse Under Milkwood returned a positive swab to cobalt after a race at Devonport. The horse recorded a reading of 19,000 micrograms per litre in urine, the highest recorded in the world. The allowable level of cobalt in Australia at the time was 200 m/pl with the previous highest level being 6470 mg/l returned by a horse trained in NSW by Darren Smith. Smith was subsequently found guilty under various rules of racing resulting in him receiving a 15-year disqualification.

Rhodes' case dragged on for several months before being heard by Tasmanian stewards as there was some discrepancy over the variation in the levels of reserve samples which produced readings of between 14,000 and 19,000 mg/l in urine. Rhodes eventually faced an inquiry at which he was found guilty of breaking three rules pertaining to the one swab and was disqualified for a total of five years.

Mick was keen for The Cleaner to tackle the Group 1 Australian Cup over 2000 metres at Flemington in the early autumn so he set about mapping out a program that would include one lead-up run in Tasmania before making the trip across Bass Strait.

With the 2015 Tasmanian Summer Racing Carnival coming to a close with only Launceston Cup day remaining on the last Wednesday in February, Mick accepted for the weight-for-age George Adams Plate, a Listed race over 1600 metres carrying prizemoney of $100,000; this was the race he had won so convincingly the previous year.

The committee of the Tasmania Turf Club were probably doing cartwheels behind closed doors when they realised they had Tasmania's cult hero on hand to help promote their premier race day with the George Adams to be promoted as a match race between the The Cleaner and the up and coming three-year-old star Admiral.

The massive crowd had just witnessed the Mick Kent-trained mare Epingle complete the Hobart-Launceston Cup double, so the stage was set for the 'Longford Lion' to do his thing.

The Cleaner took up his usual role and jockey Steve Arnold was content to allow his charge to do what he does best but when he reached the home turn and asked The Cleaner to kick clear Brendon McCoull had Admiral poised to pounce, five wide and ready to unleash.

The Cleaner found plenty as always and for a fleeting moment it looked as if he might have the youngster's measure but this time the lion was to be tamed as Barry Campbell's rising champion cruised to the front to win comfortably. Mick wasn't worried about the first-up loss; after all he had an Australian Cup appointment ahead of him. The owners appeared to be more concerned as they made their way to the enclosure, but looks can be deceiving. When the horse strolled into the runner's up stall the smiles appeared, especially when jockey Arnold gave the horse the thumbs up.

"I knew Admiral was a great three-year-old," said Mick, "probably the best we've had in Tassie for a long time, but I'd be lying if I said I didn't think my horse was going to win. But in this game you have to always be prepared to take results for what they're worth and I've learnt never to make any judgments or decisions straight after a race."

Back at the stables that night Mick spent a half-hour with his horse making sure all was right. After a mandatory inspection of his legs, and the nearside front in particular, he was content The Cleaner had escaped unscathed. Mick had identified a slight suspensory issue with The Cleaner in his nearside front leg after he ran in the previous year's JRA Cup and needed to be mindful of any soreness in that joint. He was careful with the amount and type of trackwork he gave the horse leading up to each race.

THE Group 1 Australian Cup over 2000 metres at Flemington had been on Mick's radar for some time. It was on the way home to Tasmania after the horse contested the Cox Plate that he first made mention of it. The Cleaner's training regime would be altered slightly to match the Cox Plate preparation.

The horse had a great record over the trip at Moonee Valley but a 2000-metre race at Flemington would require something else, owing to the layout of the track and the much longer home straight that could find him out at the business end. Mick decided to increase the horse's work in the week following the George Adams and then keep the routine as he had done for the Cox Plate in the week leading up to the Flemington race. The extra work was just a slight tweaking but enough to make a difference. At least, that was his thinking.

The autumn campaign was only to be two or three runs but deep down Mick was hoping it would last only two; a win in the Australian Cup would be enough to send the gelding to the paddock with a Group 1 finally in the locker.

This trip to Melbourne was made without much fuss and that suited Mick and Vern Poke whose truck Mick relied on to transport The Cleaner wherever he needed to be. By now Poke was feeling just as much a part of the show as the trainer and the horse's owners. He would organise his business around when The Cleaner was to race interstate. He also had the sides of his truck painted with a big black stripe and a sky blue stripe above it to replicate the horse's racing colours.

"I loved being a part of the show," he said. "Mick and I have become great mates over the years and I was rapt when he finally had a horse good enough to play with the big boys. I helped Mick as much as I could. When we got to Pine Lodge I'd get the horse sorted out while Mick took a breather because his lungs are buggered and he needed someone there to help out and I think he liked me doing it because he trusted me with the horse."

Despite his great record, punters were wary of The Cleaner's chances in the Cup, and he eased from an opening quote of $20 to start at $26. Happy Trails was the punter's pick at $4, with the Melbourne Cup winner of the previous spring, Protectionist second elect at $4.40. The great Cup horse, Red Cadeaux went out at $12. There was a flood of money for the David Hayes and Tom Dabernig-trained Spillway who tumbled in from $21 to $13. The Cup was run as most had forecast, with The Cleaner rolling to the front early and then waiting for the swoopers to come and run him down. The horse settled well while the favourite was back in the field of 16. Arnold called on The Cleaner to increase the tempo at the

600 metres and he responded well, but halfway up the home straight it was evident that the Tasmanian was starting to feel the pinch.

Spillway had spotted The Cleaner a dozen lengths before straightening for the long run home but jockey Michael Walker managed to steer him through tiny openings when it counted to find a clear path to the line. He hit the front 100 metres out and fought off a late bid from his $101 stablemate Extra Zero who failed to grab him by the narrowest of margins. Happy Trails was a close-up third, with The Cleaner holding on for fourth and a cheque of $45,000.

It seemed going to the well once too often was becoming a bit of a habit for the horse's owners who all but insisted Mick nominate The Cleaner for the 2000m Group 3 Easter Cup to be run at Caulfield three weeks after the Australian Cup. Their view was the field wouldn't be strong, but Mick knew his mate was starting to feel the strain. The Cleaner started second favourite at $3.60 with Sertorius the elect at $3.50. There was good money for Escado ($6.50/$6) one of the unlucky runners in the G3 Blamey Stakes over 1600m at Flemington at his previous start. The Cleaner led but again he fell short of the mark and weakened to finish fifth just over two lengths from the winner. He did have one win: the $3750 for fifth place took his prizemoney over the magic million dollar mark.

The campaign had been a profitable one but there was unrest in the camp. Mick's health had taken a nosedive a number of times leading up to and during the previous two campaigns so Bill Fawdry led the charge to discuss what might be the best for the horse. The owners had already failed in one attempt to shake Mick loose as trainer, based primarily on them doubting that Mick was healthy enough to deal with all the travelling and extra pressure of racing at Group level. That issue was about to raise its head again.

24

Another Shot at Glory

MICK was mindful that The Cleaner would be an eight-year-old come August but even though he had had only 49 starts, of which 10 of his previous dozen starts had been in Listed or Group races—in three states—the horse seemed as bright as ever. But Mick wasn't content with how the horse was performing on the training track. Not that he was lethargic, he just didn't have that special something in his demeanour that he had shown in the past.

"I've known this horse nearly all his life and I can tell straight up if something's not right with him. He's been crook a couple of times and each time I've been able to pick up on it straight away and I've been able to fix it but I couldn't quite put my finger on the problem this time around and it bothered me."

It was Fawdry who had suggested to Mick that maybe David Quinn, who had broken in the horse as a yearling, should be brought in as the horse's main trackwork rider. Mick was happy he had a competent rider to make sure the horse was doing all that was required as he worked towards finding a spot in another Cox Plate. He felt confident enough in the rider to expect him to pick up anything the horse was doing in his work that might help Mick identify any problems.

The Cleaner's second Cox Plate campaign would begin differently from the last with the G2 P.B. Lawrence Stakes (WFA) over 1400 metres at Caulfield selected to kick off his campaign. Mourinho, another eight-year-old, also was being aimed at another Cox Plate campaign for his trainer Peter Gelagotis, who trains out of a magnificent complex at Moe in Victoria's Gippsland region.

Mourinho was sensationally left out of the 2014 Cox Plate field after the Moonee Valley Racing Club used its discretionary power to include Gai Waterhouse's three-year-old Wandjina ahead of Gelagotis' well-performed middle distance performer. Gelagotis was fuming and when interviewed after the final field had been declared he told prominent Victorian racing writer Brad Waters: "I think if people go home and read the form guide, they'll be surprised our horse is not in the final field of 14."

Two weeks out from the Lawrence Stakes The Cleaner's trackwork had improved to the point where Mick was happy that he had the horse back to where he needed him to be to continue with another ambitious campaign. Although he was hoping to win the Lawrence Stakes, his main aim was winning another Dato Tan Chin Nam Stakes as that would guarantee the horse another start in the Cox Plate. Noel Callow had been on the phone to Mick to tell him he was back in Australia and that he was available to ride The Cleaner. Steve Arnold had done nothing wrong on the horse, but Mick had such a huge regard for Callow, he booked him for the upcoming campaign.

"There have been two riders who I reckon suited The Cleaner better than all the others and they were Noel Callow and Jason Maskiell. I couldn't go with Maskiell because he'd been done for drugs use, so when Callow rang I didn't take too much convincing. I called Steve to tell him what I'd done and he was okay with that. Well at least he said he was."

THE Cleaner looked magnificent as he entered the mounting yard at Caulfield for his first run back from the spell. His coat was gleaming and he seemed to have grown another hand from his last campaign. He would leave the gates from barrier six in the field of nine and with no other genuine speed in the race he was assured of leading.

But missing from the picture was his trainer. Mick had succumbed to a bad bout of the flu. "I'd been fighting the flu for days and I knew if I travelled to Melbourne I'd only do myself more damage so I asked Quinny if he wanted to take the horse and he jumped at the chance. He'd been riding the horse in trackwork and he was getting along with him and my stable foreman couldn't make the trip. I thought David was our best option."

Diehard punters are always looking for an edge and as Mick had been gracious enough to explain the issues he had with The Cleaner early in his preparation, it wasn't surprising that he was allowed to go around a $10 chance with the Wez Hunter-trained Smokin' Joey, winner of the Group 3 Bletchingly Stakes over 1200 metres at Caulfield at his previous start, sent out the $4.20 favourite.

Callow followed the well-written script and sent The Cleaner straight to the front and the race went as expected until Mourinho arrived late to spoil the party, getting up in the last stride to win by the narrowest of margins.

The owners were delighted with his first-up run and when Callow got off he almost apologised for finishing second. When he slid from the saddle in the enclosure Callow looked at the owners and told them that the horse wouldn't be beaten at his next start. That was music to their ears. Everyone walked away from the defeat with a smile. Mick was on the phone to Fawdry and he reported what Callow had told them. Mick had a smirk on his face that suggested the owners had just been the recipients of some well-delivered lip service.

"One thing I've learned over the years is to take a jockey's opinion with a grain of salt," he said. Most of them will tell you anything to keep a ride and to stop you from thinking they're dickheads. Unless you have a really good idea of how to read a race they'll get away with murder but I've become a wake-up to them so they don't try and lay too much on me these days."

Before The Cleaner's next shot at the Dato, the horse's connections were looking forward to the Tasmanian Racing Awards dinner to be held at the Country Club Resort in Launceston, a week before his next start. The Cleaner was favourite to win the Tasmanian Horse Of The Year and he was a unanimous choice. The talented three-year-old Admiral was voted best in his age group, with his win over The Cleaner in the George Adams the best of his three wins in Tasmania. He finished a game fifth in the Group 1 Australian Guineas at Flemington, won by Wandjina.

When it came time for an acceptance speech The Cleaner's owners ventured to the stage but surprisingly it was Paul Burt who was selected to accept the award.

Under normal circumstances awards night host Colin McNiff has control of all the interviews by keeping a firm grip on the microphone so as to prevent over-enthusiastic award winners from doing what Burt was about to do. Burt had spied a roving wireless microphone perched helplessly on a nearby lectern and as it was already switched on, he proceeded to fumble his way through an acceptance speech that was best forgotten. One expletive slipping out might be acceptable but three or more times is unforgiveable. Mick, who had also received an award that night for his services to the industry, primarily for the way he had handled himself and the horse during their escapades interstate, was embarrassed by what Burt had to say.

"I was ashamed after the acceptance speech. I use that sort of language when I'm knocking about the stables but I'd never let one slip while talking in public and especially when there are women in the room. I felt sick in the guts when he started dropping the F-bomb and I was so embarrassed I left the function as soon as I told Paul what I thought of his speech."

To his credit Burt subsequently apologised to anyone who would listen for how he handled himself. Having never spoken in public before it was probably a grave error of the team to give him the responsibility in the first place.

BUT all was forgotten by the time the group travelled to Melbourne for the Dato and Callow's words from Caulfield were still ringing in their ears. But this time the jockey was spot-on in his assessment. The Cleaner, a $5.50 shot, led, and despite hitting a flat spot about 500 metres from home, he turned a length in front and hit the line almost two lengths clear of Bagman and Dibayani with another Tasmanian-bred gelding, Kenjorwood, an eye-catching fourth. Mick had done what many thought was an impossible task off such a short preparation. The Cleaner had clinched another berth in the Cox Plate. Fixed odds bookmakers acted swiftly after the win by slashing his Cox Plate odds from $51 to $21.

This win, his fifth at the Valley, was The Cleaner's most emphatic and he delivered the knockout blow to his rivals by running his last 400 metres in a sizzling 21.9 seconds. And it wasn't as if he beat substandard opposition. He had thrashed another hot field including a number of Cox Plate aspirants looking to stake their claims for a berth in the weight-for-age championship of Australasia.

When The Cleaner entered the home straight with a commanding lead race caller Greg Miles' tone sharpened as the horse extended his lead 200 metres out, with Miles delivering a comment that summed up the effort: "The Cleaner is treating his rivals with contempt". Miles is a self-confessed fan of The Cleaner and on a number of occasions he's made no apology for his obvious affection for the Tasmanian frontrunner.

"There's always an extra element of excitement when The Cleaner is in a race," he said, "and I guess it has something to do with how strong and how different a horse has to be when they race the way The Cleaner races. Leaders tend to have that little bit more of the X-factor about them as Vo Rogue and Sunline did when they were at their very best.

"It's one of the toughest things in racing to do it all from the front and I'm sure it is his racing style that has endeared him to the racing public, especially in Melbourne. But when you add the Mick Burles story behind The Cleaner we had a recipe for a typical rags to riches tale. We know how much Australians love underdogs and Mick and The Cleaner filled that bill."

Calling some of The Cleaner's early races kept Miles on his toes but when he understood fully the horse's ability to keep going when under pressure, he was able to describe more accurately how the horse was travelling.

"I learned very quickly that he was a tough horse to judge how well he was going," said Miles. "He would often hit flat spots in a race and he'd look like he was struggling. He'd be five lengths clear at the half-mile and the next time you're calling him he's a length in front so you'd think they've probably got him. But getting to him was one thing, getting past him was another. He's never been one of those fly along leaders who puncture. He just had an enormous ability to sustain a run for a long, long way. He was a tricky horse to call in that regard but I learned very quickly you don't write him off."

He added: "The Cleaner was never in the same league as our A grade Group 1 horses but what he did have was incredible popular appeal and that probably places him above many other horses who have better race records. It didn't matter whether he was the favourite or a 20-1 shot, people loved him for how he raced and the story behind him.

"That he travelled over by boat from Tassie every time was another factor that saw him defy the odds because it is almost unheard of for a horse to travel the way he did, and so often, yet he was still able to match it with the best in Group races. It is no wonder he captured the imagination of so many and you can't help but admire a horse that consistently showed such bravery. A little part of me was cheering for him more often that not.

"As for Mick, well, he is one of the great characters of the game and without him alongside the horse The Cleaner probably wouldn't have been such a phenomenon. Mick was always happy to talk to the media and he brought something different to each interview. He was always very quotable and he was certainly entertaining."

THE previous year The Cleaner's path to the Cox Plate included the JRA Cup at Moonee Valley as his final lead-up race but a change to the race program saw the JRA Cup scheduled a week later than normal and that didn't suit Mick, so he chose a less conservative path and eyed off the $402,000 Group 1 Underwood Stakes at Caulfield over 1800 metres as the horse's entrée to the main course.

The Cleaner had failed at his first attempt on the Caulfield track but that was when he was with Robert Smerdon and at the end of a four-start campaign that eventually led to the owners sending the horse back to Mick to train. But a more recent effort at Caulfield in the Easter Cup, in which he finished fifth beaten only 2-1/2 lengths, had encouraged Mick to pursue any race at Caulfield that might suit his Cox Plate preparation. The horse's excellent first-up effort in the Lawrence Stakes at Caulfield also convinced Mick the Underwood would fit perfectly into the program.

"I couldn't believe how well the horse looked after his second Dato win," he said. "When we got home after the race he really blossomed. He was bigger in the bum, bigger in the shoulder, just bigger all over. He's always been a powerfully-built bastard but this time in he really filled out."

The Underwood boasted a star cast including Mourinho, who was fast becoming The Cleaner's arch enemy number one, Fawkner, who was again heading to the Cox Plate and the major cups and then there was Mongolian Khan, the four-year-old bred in Tasmania by Graeme McCulloch who had taken all before him the previous season winning the New Zealand Derby and Australian Derby.

When Mick first assessed the field he had some reservations about whether The Cleaner could overcome his Caulfield hoodoo but after further study and based on the sectional times he knew his horse was capable of his confidence grew and by race start time he said: "If he can't win this race today he probably can't win the Cox Plate."

The Cleaner finished third in a three-way photo-finish of veterans with Mourinho gaining the judge's verdict by a nose from Fawkner with The Cleaner a nose away. It was a brilliant finish and one that had race caller Miles gasping for air as the trio crossed the line almost as one. It was all the more remarkable to think the three geldings were all eight-year-olds, fighting to the death in a Group 1.

ALL Mick had to do now was play out time and keep his horse ticking over. But just after he returned to Tasmania, The Cleaner's trackwork rider was starting to take control of things a tad more than the trainer would have liked. If that wasn't upsetting enough, Mick's emphysema had been causing him sleepless nights and the added pressure of gearing up for another Cox Plate was also weighing him down.

"I was starting to get annoyed with Quinny (trackwork rider David Quinn) because he started barking orders and making suggestions of what I should be doing with the horse. I wasn't about to cop that so I told him to mind his own business and just stick to riding trackwork and stop trying to be the trainer. It was the last thing I wanted with a Cox Plate less than a month away."

But the Cox Plate wasn't the only big race on the radar. Mick had been contacted by the Gold Coast Turf Club about the prospects of The Cleaner heading north to tackle the $1 million Stayers Cup over 1800 metres in early January. With plans to head to another Australian Cup in the Autumn, Mick thought the Gold Coast race would fit perfectly into the horse's program. The Stayers Cup is one of nine races on Magic Millions Day of which five carry prizemoney of $1 million with the 3YO Guineas worth $2 million and the 2YO Classic offering a stake of $2.5 million.

The Cox Plate has always boasted the cream of Australasia's middle distance performers with the odd champion dominating as So You Think did the second time around in 2010 as a four-year-old and who could forget Sunline's consecutive wins in 1999 and 2000 or Northerly's back-to-back efforts in 2001-02. Mick knew he had only an outside chance of standing in the winner's circle after the Plate but he kept reminding himself of the old adage—if you're not in it you can't win it.

Mick was more nervous this time around than at his first attempt even though he had Callow on top and the horse had drawn perfectly in barrier two. He led the field comfortably but when he reached the half-way mark Callow was niggling at his mount and Mick knew immediately something wasn't right with the horse. When they approached the home turn The Cleaner started to hang out badly and on straightening Callow was unable to get the horse anywhere near the rails. He finished seventh to earn $100,000 prizemoney that well and truly covered expenses but that he finished almost 11 lengths from the record-breaking winner Winx was of great concern to his trainer.

The team travelled home without as much as a whimper from the media but Mick was pleased to have peace and quiet so he could get down to finding the problem that had caused Bill to hang out so badly. A basic vet's examination failed to find any structural damage but when the horse's blood tests came back it revealed a virus of some description that was accompanied by mucus dripping from the horse's nostrils the day after they arrived back home. An elevated temperature didn't surprise either the vet or Mick.

"I had the horse treated with antibiotics and after a few days he'd come good but we were coming up empty on why the horse had hung so badly. I had the chiropractor to him and he found nothing out of order."

Mick had decided to nominate The Cleaner for the WFA Conquering Stakes over 1400 metres under lights in Launceston six weeks after his Cox Plate flop. The relationship between trackwork rider Quinn and Mick had not improved greatly since the trainer had laid down the law as to who was responsible for training the horse.

Quinn has a passion for thoroughbreds and when he was offered the opportunity to be a part of Then Cleaner's journey he jumped at it. After all he had broken the horse in and had watched his career carefully. "When I started to ride the horse in trackwork I quickly identified all of his assets," Quinn said. "He is a brick, as tough as they come and even in his trackwork you can feel the toughness. But he also is such a wonderful horse to be around. There's not a mean bone in his body and while he mucks about when he's in the stables, once he gets on the track it's all business and I reckon that's what sets him apart from most of the rest."

As the Conquering Stakes approached, there was no sign of the virus that had hit the horse's blood count. If Mick had thought there was any doubt as to his fitness, the horse would have stayed in his box.

"The more I analysed the situation with the horse the more I came to the conclusion that he should probably be retired at the end of his prep. He'd won close to $1.4 million so he had been a very nice investment for the owners and given what he'd done there might never be a better time to pull the pin and let him retire on a good note and not after breaking down.

"If the cause of him hanging in his races could be identified then we could deal with it and then look at racing him on but as it was there needed to be proper scans and things done to make doubly sure we knew what the problem was. All I could do was take advice from my vet and ensure that whatever we did, it would be in the horse's best interests."

In the days leading up to the Conquering Stakes, The Cleaner had shown no signs of faltering in his trackwork and blood tests returned a clean bill of health so Mick accepted him for the race. As the horse was being led around the mounting yard prior to the race, the word had spread that all might not be well in The Cleaner camp and that resulted in the now four-year-old Admiral firming in from $3 to $2.50. The Cleaner was still an odds-on prospect but his price had eased from $1.30 to $1.60.

Callow urged The Cleaner from the gates and he was just about to roll to the front when one of the rank outsiders, One Shot Off, moved alongside with apprentice Shiralee Maher aboard and when she looked across at Callow to signal her intentions Callow obliged by letting her take her mount to the lead. Callow had The Cleaner on a tight rein three then five lengths off the leader but when he asked for an effort 600 metres out he had little to give. When Brendon McCoull released the reins on Admiral, who had been cruising in fourth spot on the rails, the end result was a foregone conclusion. Admiral won comfortably from Geegees Goldengirl and potential Cups candidate Player One who rattled home. The Cleaner struggled home to finish second-last only just in advance of the tearaway leader One Shot Off.

The winner was now being praised as the heir apparent to The Cleaner as the state's best horse, a judgment rated laughable by fans of The Cleaner, given what the horse had achieved at Group level.

But there were ructions back at The Cleaner's stall with Quinn screaming that Mick had done the wrong thing by running the horse in the Conquering. Inside a week Bill Fawdry was on Mick's doorstep telling him the horse was being taken from him and that The Cleaner would be heading interstate to be trained by Mourinho's trainer Peter Gelagotis at Moe.

25

The Tears Flow

THE news of the split spread like wildfire and the media frenzy that followed had the owners ducking for cover. Not only had Fawdry, Burt and Lowish ripped the heart out of the trainer, they had broken a partnership that had put Tasmanian racing back on the map. Mick had prepared the horse to win more than $1.3 million in prizemoney and he had done it while training the horse out of his home state.

Social media went berserk with some of the tweets on Twitter causing the owners to go to ground. The local media spent the day queuing up for interviews with Mick and interstate media also were all over the bust up. After Mick had given his version to Melbourne's Radio Sport National on why the horse had been taken from him, Fawdry joined the host of the program to deliver his side of the story.

Mick was angry and lashed out at the owners but in between radio, press and television interviews he sat back in his dilapidated easy chair in his shipping container-like dwelling and sobbed over the loss of his best mate.

"I cried myself to sleep the night they took him away. I'm not normally a person who shows his emotion but it has always been different with this horse. I don't know what it was but whenever anyone asked me why I get emotional about him, my eyes well up and the tears start. I guess it's because I really love him. At the end of the day, they own the horse and are entitled to do whatever they like with him—that's racing. But when they all sit back in a few years' time and have a good look at what went on I hope they realise that they did the wrong thing. It's not as if they needed the money."

Fawdry's RSN interview confirmed what most people were thinking about the owners' decision to take the horse from Mick. But he had a resolve not to air any dirty laundry in public. Whatever was the main reason for them moving the horse would remain guarded and known only to Mick and the three owners. At least that was the original plan.

Fawdry told the author: "People would be amazed if they knew all the reasons why we felt we had to take the horse off Mick but we think enough of Mick to not go public with them. But I think his health was definitely one of the main reasons we thought the horse would be better off with someone else. I couldn't get that visit to the hospital out of my head.

"To see Mick lying there and hearing that he couldn't get his lungs fixed because he was still smoking. At one stage we thought he might not be around for much longer and that he might have been making big decisions about the horse when he wasn't in the right frame of mind.

"But once we'd made our minds up to take the horse off Mick we felt much better about the future. Peter Gelagotis has a very good setup at Moe and the horse was going to get the best if he needed any treatments. But here in Tasmania, Mick was very restricted with what he had access to.

"At Peter's they could swim the horse regularly and put him on a treadmill anytime if needed but there was none of that with Mick. I reckon the horse will give us another 12 months at least, the way he is going to be looked after and that's not what he had to look forward to if he stayed with Mick, because he wanted to retire the horse."

Owners can have short memories and that may have applied in this instance, after all, The Cleaner, under Mick's guidance, delivered so much without having access to the things that Fawdry had listed. But the niggling issue Mick had with his stablehand David Quinn most likely stemmed from an arrangement Quinn had with Fawdry.

Said Fawdry: "David (Quinn) was virtually Mick's foreman and I admit I started to get David to report back to me on what was going on at the stables as far as The Cleaner was concerned. I was of the opinion that it was part of a stable foreman's responsibilities to tell owners anything they wanted to know about their horse so I saw no wrong in what I was doing.

"The night The Cleaner ran so badly in Launceston, David told us that he had told Mick not to run him because the horse wasn't right and Mick's response was that he was running because he needed the money. That was the main reason why we ended up taking the horse off Mick."

Mick did not deny he had made those comments to Quinn. "Quinny was ranting on about the horse not being right but I'd had the horse's bloods done and they were perfect. He told me I should scratch the horse and I said no and then he said why—so to shut him up I said because I wanted the money. I knew that would be the end of it (the conversation). Nobody knew if the horse had any muscular or skeletal problems and I certainly wouldn't have run him if I thought there were any issues. It was just my bad luck that I'd made that comment and then the horse went out and ran nearly last."

THE day after The Cleaner left Mick's stables, Mick was at the doctor's surgery to collect a new prescription when his phone rang. It was Peter Gelagotis. Mick didn't answer, switched the phone off and did not turn it on again that day. It would be two days before Mick was back in the communication game and when he turned the phone on he had more than 100 missed calls registered on his old flip-top mobile. Within the blink of an eye they were all deleted.

"I had to pull the pin on the phone interviews because every time someone asked me about the horse I had to relive the bust up all over again. I knew the interest would eventually die down but it was a bastard waiting for that to happen. The hardest thing to deal with was having to walk past Bill's empty box at feed time. It was even worse when I looked into his empty paddock. By the time I got back inside I'd have tears rolling down my face. It was horrible."

The Gelagotis stable was also feeling the heat. Peter and the stable's manager, brother Manny, had been in constant contact with Mick trying to patch things up to make the transition to their stable as smooth as possible.

Galegotis finally understood that Mick was not going to see the horse off with his blessing. As a final carrot to sweeten the split he offered to allow The Cleaner to run in Mick's colours but the Tasmanian wasn't having a bar of it.

"Why would I let them use my colours? They must have thought I'd come down in the last shower. The only reason they wanted to use my colours was so that if the horse raced in Melbourne again they might not get as much flak if everyone thought the horse had moved on with my blessing. Peter asked me a few things about the horse and for the sake of the horse's welfare I told him what he wanted to know but that's as far as I was going to help out."

However, Fawdry came up with a clever solution, by registering a new set of colours—black body and sleeves with sky blue hoops and cap—similar to Mick's racing silks.

"We wanted to have a similar set of colours so that he still looked like the same horse in his races," said Fawdry. "The people who support the horse are used to seeing the colours that the jockeys wore when he last raced, so when Mick rejected the offer to use his colours we thought we'd get our own. We had trouble getting new colours registered until I spoke to this fellow from Racing Victoria who said he could fix everything. The next thing we know he's come up with a design and they are the ones we had registered. They have more blue on them than Mick's but they are very similar."

THE Gelagotis stable was still keen to have Mick involved in some way so Peter came up with the idea of having Mick attend race meetings at which The Cleaner was to appear and at the stable's expense. Although that appeared an extremely kind gesture it cut Mick to the quick.

"I know Peter Gelagotis meant well when he offered to have me be there to see the horse race, but why on earth would I want to put myself through that ordeal? It would only make me relive the bust up over and over again and at the end of the race meetings I wouldn't be able to bring the horse home.

"After that offer I told them all (the owners and the trainer) not to include me in anything that concerned The Cleaner in the future and that if I wanted to get involved I'd be happy to just watch his races on TV."

Peter Gelagotis had the horse about two months and after having the horse's legs scanned it was revealed Bill had a small lesion in his near-front suspensory ligament, the same leg Mick had been keeping an eye on for the previous two years.

The only remedy was rest and a moderate treatment plan, which Gelagotis put in place. The Cleaner returned to the track in a blaze of glory, winning a trial at Cranbourne by six lengths on July 15, 2016, almost seven months after his run in the Conquering, the longest break in a career that had stretched back to February 2011. He resumed with another shot in the G2 P.B. Lawrence at Caulfield on August 13, showing all his customary dash, although attacked in the lead throughout. Although he finished 11th of 14, Steve Arnold, back in charge, did not knock him about at the end, and he was just 3.5 lengths from the winner, Miss Rose De Lago.

WHEN The Cleaner left Mick's yard the trainer had only four other horses to work. One of them, Triple Bee, belonged to Paul Burt and Mick had a quarter share in it. A week later Triple Bee left Mick's stables after they had settled up for the share. Mick was now down to three. There weren't many options open to him other than to try and find more horses to train, although when The Cleaner left, the trainer's enthusiasm was at an all-time low.

"I was determined not to let losing The Cleaner ruin my life. I was very upset and I had every right to feel sorry for myself because I'd lost my best mate, but I've been through some serious shit in my life and this was just another episode I had to deal with and move on. Some things are harder than others to overcome and this was a big hurdle but I know where the horse is if I ever want to see him so I had to get on with my life because moping about wasn't going to get the horse back."

Mick's way of moving on was to attend the 2016 Tasmanian Magic Millions Yearling Sale where he was hoping lightning might strike again. He spent a week poring over the catalogue and came up with a couple he thought might suit his budget. Then, out of the blue, he received a phone call from a Melbourne businessman who asked if Mick would be interested in attending the sale to buy him a horse.

"Bill Sutcliffe, a nice fella, rang me about buying a yearling so we discussed a budget and I went to the sale hoping to pick up another bargain but the prices were surprisingly high compared to previous years, although that was probably expected because the standard of the yearlings was better.

"I ended up buying a real nice filly by Anacheeva out of Aprilia, a terrific race mare trained by Dave Brunton. She was placed in a Bow Mistress. I paid $27,000 for her and I reckon we got her cheap. Bill was rapt when he saw her and she's already named—Clean Acheever. I also bought a colt by Needs Further from Inchcape and paid $8000 for him. He's been syndicated out so I have two really nice two-year-olds to play with."

MICK won't miss the high life or rubbing shoulders with the best in the business. He's always been a bloke who lives for the day and nothing will ever change his ways. He will survive on his disability pension of $1900 a month, of which about a third goes on stable rent, and as long as he's capable of putting a bridle on a horse he will go to bed at night happy with his lot in life. He's been a chef, a truck driver, fruit picker, labourer, street sweeper and a share farmer but the one profession that has taken him on the ride of his life will always remain his greatest love.

If there was such a thing as time travel and Mick Burles was offered the chance to go back to where it all began and change the path that led him to where he is today, the craggy-faced trainer with a wicked sense of humour would probably have a chuckle to himself and say, 'no thanks, piss off'.

At 67 and suffering from emphysema that requires him to be on oxygen more often than not, Mick says he's not afraid of dying. He knows it's coming sooner than later. With his best mate now being cared for by another, Mick knows he has to refill the tank and move on. But the truth is, Mick and The Cleaner are engaged in a race nobody wants to win. An unofficial market has been framed and Mick is the odds on favourite to be the first to find the line.

When Mick was told that The Cleaner was being taken from him, he asked if he could have the horse back when he had finished racing. But he was told that the horse had been promised to Armidale Stud, at Carrick, out of Launceston, to act as a 'grandfather' to the young horses on the property. The proposition was put to The Cleaner's part-owner Bill Fawdry by Armidale's general manager Robyn Whishaw when the horse was making his mark in Group races in Melbourne in 2015 and the deal was done. Fawdry remains adamant there would be no changes to the plan.

While Mick will be able to visit his best mate whenever he likes at Armidale, only a 10-minute drive from Mick's stables at Longford, a more permanent arrangement has already been put in place for Mick and Bill. When The Cleaner's life is over he will be buried at Armidale with a special plot put aside and a gravestone that will highlight his racing achievements. Whishaw was only too pleased to grant Mick's wish: when his time comes his ashes will be scattered on The Cleaner's grave so that they will be reunited forever.

The Cleaner's Record

	DATE	RACECOURSE	RACE NAME	GROUP/ LISTED	JOCKEY	PRIZEMONEY ($)
11th	13-Aug-16	Caulfield	P. B. Lawrence Stakes WFA	G2	Steven Arnold	
7th	09-Dec-15	Mowbray	Mitsubishi Conquering Wfa	LR	Noel Callow	2000
7th	24-Oct-15	Moonee Valley	William Hill Cox Plate	G1	Noel Callow	100000
3rd	26-Sep-15	Caulfield	Underwood Stakes	G1	Noel Callow	36000
1st	05-Sep-15	Moonee Valley	Dato' Tan Chin Nam Stakes	G2	Noel Callow	151500
2nd	15-Aug-15	Caulfield	Back To Caul. Lawrence Stakes	G2	Noel Callow	36000
5th	04-Apr-15	Caulfield	Le Pine Funerals Easter Cup	G3	Steven Arnold	3750
4th	14-Mar-15	Flemington	Australian Cup	G1	Steven Arnold	45000
2nd	25-Feb-15	Mowbray	Tattsbet George Adams Plate	LR	Steven Arnold	18000
9th	22-Nov-14	Ascot	Railway Stakes	G1	Steven Arnold	
3rd	08-Nov-14	Flemington	Emirates Stakes	G1	Steven Arnold	90000
9th	25-Oct-14	Moonee Valley	W.S. Cox Plate	G1	Steven Arnold	
1st	26-Sep-14	Moonee Valley	Alternate Railway Jra Cup	G3	Steven Arnold	121500

	DATE	RACECOURSE	RACE NAME	GROUP/ LISTED	JOCKEY	PRIZEMONEY ($)
1st	06-Sep-14	Moonee Valley	Dato' Tan Chin Nam Stakes	G2	Steven Arnold	151500
1st	02-Aug-14	Moonee Valley	Jeep Don't Hold Back Hcp		Noel Callow	48000
2nd	12-Jul-14	Flemington	Vrc-Crv Winter C'ship Final	LR	Anthony Darmanin	27000
1st	21-Jun-14	Moonee Valley	Dominant Travis Harrison Cup		Anthony Darmanin	48000
2nd	24-May-14	Flemington	Vrc-Crv Winter C'ship Ht		Anthony Darmanin	14400
1st	26-Feb-14	Mowbray	Tattsbet George Adams Plate	LR	Anthony Darmanin	60000
5th	14-Feb-14	Elwick	Hobart Cup	G3	Anthony Darmanin	5625
2nd	02-Feb-14	Elwick	Programmed Turnpoint J.C. Cup		Anthony Darmanin	9000
2nd	18-Jan-14	Flemington	Piping Lane Hcp		Anthony Darmanin	14400
2nd	31-Dec-13	Mowbray	R W Trinder Qlty		Anthony Darmanin	5000
6th	21-Dec-13	Elwick	Kevin Sharkie Tasmanian Stakes	LR	Darren Gauci	1800
3rd	20-Nov-13	Mowbray	Tasmanian T.C. Newmarket Hcp	LR	Darren Gauci	8100
11th	31-Aug-13	Caulfield	Heatherlie Handicap	LR	Jason Maskiell	
3rd	03-Aug-13	Moonee Valley	Handicap		Brodie Loy	9000
5th	20-Jul-13	Flemington	Handicap		Jason Maskiell	2500

	DATE	RACECOURSE	RACE NAME	GROUP/ LISTED	JOCKEY	PRIZEMONEY ($)
11th	06-Jul-13	Flemington	Winter Championship	LR	Craig Newitt	
1st	22-Jun-13	Flemington	David Bourke Provincial Plate		Jason Maskiell	62500
7th	27-Feb-13	Mowbray	Aami Launceston Cup	G3	Jason Maskiell	4500
2nd	10-Feb-13	Elwick	Aami Hobart Cup	G3	Jason Maskiell	40500
1st	20-Jan-13	Elwick	Betfair Summer Cup		Jason Maskiell	16250
10th	09-Jan-13	Devonport	Simons Design Devonport Cup		Jason Maskiell	
1st	02-Jan-13	Mowbray	Field Family Qlty Hcp		Jason Maskiell	13000
1st	16-Dec-12	Elwick	Kevin Sharkie Tasmanian Stakes	LR	Jason Maskiell	54000
5th	29-Sep-12	Mornington	R.M. Ansett Classic	LR	Ben Knobel	3000
1st	29-Aug-12	Sandown (L)	Metro Solar Hcp (89)		Ben Knobel	21001
2nd	04-Aug-12	Moonee Valley	Hong Kong Racehorse Owners Hcp		Craig Newitt	18000
1st	22-Jul-12	Elwick	Gee Gee Horse Stud Open Hcp		Shannon Brazil	10075
1st	08-Jul-12	Elwick	Fuji Xerox Tasmania Hcp		Shannon Brazil	10075
7th	11-Jan-12	Devonport	Simons Design Devonport Cup		Stephen Maskiell	2000

	DATE	RACECOURSE	RACE NAME	GROUP/ LISTED	JOCKEY	PRIZEMONEY ($)
1st	01-Jan-12	Longford	Elders Longford Cup		Jacques Luxe	10075
1st	11-Dec-11	Elwick	Brighton Cup		Stephen Maskiell	13000
2nd	23-Nov-11	Mowbray	Country Club Tasmania (Bm78)		Jacques Luxe	3000
2nd	25-Sep-11	Elwick	Stonemason Wines (Bm78)		Jacques Luxe	3000
1st	04-Sep-11	Devonport	Shaw Contracting (Bm78)		Jacques Luxe	9750
1st	15-Aug-11	Mowbray	Tote Tasmania (Bm68)		Jacques Luxe	7800
1st	07-Aug-11	Mowbray	The Tote Racing Ctre Plate-C1		Jacques Luxe	7800
1st	17-Jul-11	Mowbray	St Andrews Plate (C1)		Jacques Luxe	7800
2nd	26-Jun-11	Mowbray	Ttc Members Plate (C1)		Jacques Luxe	2320
5th	05-Jun-11	Elwick	Raine & Horne Plate (C1)		Cameron Quilty	
8th	26-May-11	Mowbray	Launceston Peugeot Mdn Plate		Cameron Quilty	
10th	23-Feb-11	Mowbray	Statewide Traffic Control Mdn		Kelvin Sanderson	
13th	10-Feb-11	Mowbray	Tasmanian Mdn Plate		Rasit Yetimova	
					TOTAL PRIZEMONEY ($)	$1,327,521

The Cleaner's statistics provided courtesy of Racing and Sports.